BUILT FOR GROWTH

How Builder Personality
Shapes Your Business,
Your Team, and
Your Ability to Win

BUILT FOR GROWTH

CHRIS KUENNE AND JOHN DANNER

HARVARD BUSINESS REVIEW PRESS

BOSTON, MASSACHUSETTS

Copyright 2017 Harvard Business Publishing Corporation
All rights reserved
Printed in the United States of America

10 9 8 7 6 5 4 3 2

The web addresses referenced in this book were live and correct at the time of the book's publication but may be subject to change.

Library of Congress Cataloging-in-Publication Data

Names: Kuenne, Chris, author. | Danner, John, author.
Title: Built for growth : how builder personality shapes your business, your team, and your ability to win / Chris Kuenne and John Danner.
Description: Boston, Massachusetts: Harvard Business Review Press, [2017]
Identifiers: LCCN 2016052190 | ISBN 9781633692763 (hardcover: alk. paper)
Subjects: LCSH: Businesspeople—Psychology. | Success in business. | Industrial management.
Classification: LCC BF637.S8 K84 2017 | DDC 658.4/092—dc23 LC record available at https://lccn.loc.gov/2016052190

ISBN: 9781633692763
eISBN: 9781633692770

To my sons, Peter, William, and Matthew, in the hope they will find their own building métiers, and to my daughter, Olivia, a painter of rainbows, whose memory inspires all that I seek to build.

—Chris

To Eliot, Chris, and Will, whose growth is a source of continuing joy, discovery, and pride for their mother and me.

—John

Contents

PART THREE. BECOMING THE BEST BUILDER YOU CAN BE

Strategies for Enhancing Your Impact

BUILT FOR GROWTH

1

BUILDER PERSONALITY

The Essential Force for Growth

Building for growth is *the* business imperative for every entrepreneur, leader, manager, and company. So, are you built for growth? Because who you are shapes how you build.

If you're a builder of a new business—whether you're running an independent startup or a new venture inside an existing company—you face a unique set of challenges. You must convert your ideas into products, galvanize individual talent for collaborative impact, transform buyers into partners, align financial and executive support, and elevate your business to meaningful scale. And all the while, you're fighting the status quo—often meeting powerful resistance to your new idea from people who don't get it.

We've been intrigued with these challenges—as advisers and consultants to organizations and startups, as investors in new businesses, as professors, and as business builders ourselves. Over our careers, we have shared with hundreds of management teams and thousands of Princeton and Berkeley students the principles of starting and growing new businesses, and we have made investment decisions on dozens of fast-growing startups across the market landscape. Through each of these vantage points, we are constantly amazed by the variety of paths leaders and entrepreneurs take to build successful, growing ventures.

Probably like you, we wondered if it's possible to codify the different paths of success. Who succeeds, and how? Are there hidden patterns that determine the success of building and growing a new business? How can someone get better at it?

To answer these questions, we employed a patented research methodology to better understand who builds successful new businesses and how they do so (see "Our Research Approach" in the shaded pages at the end of this chapter and Appendix A for a discussion of our research methodology). In addition, we reviewed the literature on successful entrepreneurs and conducted in-depth interviews with dozens of seasoned business builders.

Our conclusion—and the core idea on which this book is based—is that the personality of the leader or founder is *the* animating force in building any new business. That is, the particular combination of beliefs and preferences that reflects his or her motivation, decision-making mode, management approach, and leadership style. These factors play out dramatically throughout the startup and scaling of a new business. The Builder's Personality is the essential engine of shaping the team, product, and overall business—but can also be a formidable obstacle to them. Anyone involved in leading, supporting, or funding new businesses needs to understand how the force of the Builder Personality impacts the growth process.

Of course, many elements shape the success or failure of a new business, whether it's a stand-alone startup or a new venture inside a larger corporation. Regardless of the setting, both builders are engaged in "the pursuit of opportunity beyond resources controlled," as Howard Stevenson, the renowned Harvard Business School professor, defined entrepreneurship.[1] But unlike the other resources you need to successfully grow a business, personality is the one directly—and quintessentially—in your control.

This book decodes the interplay between the business founder's personality and the dynamics of growing a business. Our research has revealed four Builder Personalities, and we demonstrate how each one succeeds and fails in different ways in growing a new business. In this practical book, we provide you with tools and examples for assessing your own personality and blueprints to help you apply these ideas to grow your business, build your team, and win.

The Four Business Builder Personalities

Our research has discovered there is no single type of highly successful business builder, but rather four distinct Builder Personalities. We call them the Driver, Explorer, Crusader, and Captain. Each Builder Personality Type builds for growth in markedly different ways, based on four discriminating factors—their motivation to become an entrepreneur and their styles of decision-making mode, management approach, and leadership style. Chapters 2 through 5 discuss each of these builder personalities and give examples and stories illustrating how they work. For now, here are brief descriptions of each personality. Which one sounds most like you? After you have read these summaries of the four types, look for the section "Which Builder Personality Is Most Similar to Yours?" for guidance on deciding which personality you are most like.

The Driver:
Relentless, Commercially Focused, and Highly Confident

Drivers can't help themselves. They have to become builders of business or social ventures of their own as a means of self-validation. Entrepreneurship is almost hardwired into their very identity. They are supremely confident individuals, relentless in pursuing commercial success based on their uncanny anticipation of what markets and customers are looking for.

Drivers often don't last long as employees in other people's organizations. They eschew rules and bureaucracy, seeing them as tools to focus the average person, yet often confine the truly gifted, independent-thinking actor. Drivers are willing to do whatever it takes to realize the commercial success inherent in what they believe is their unbounded potential, in fact their destiny.

While not universally the case, the Driver often has something to prove. Perhaps he or she has been thwarted—passed over or even fired—in an earlier job. Or perhaps having grown up in modest circumstances, the Driver is fueled by a desire to apply his or her innate skills to build enormous value and, in so doing, enjoy a better life. Mark Cuban is a famous example. The son of a car upholsterer, he always believed he could and should build a stronger future for himself and, eventually, his family through his drive and innate commercialization skills.[2] This chip on a Driver's shoulder fuels an inner need to prove him or herself to others.

Drivers are not dreamers caught up in the world of ideas; they are doers, willing to outwork, outthink, and outsell anybody in their path. As Ben Weiss of Bai Brands, a new fast-growing healthy beverage company, said, "There's a tenacity to who I am, that gave birth to this product . . . I'm the most persistent guy in the world. I don't pretend to be the smartest guy in the room. Everyone has ideas—I just take them a little further than most people. And then when they fail, I don't get disillusioned. I just pick up the pieces and keep going."[3]

However, the Drivers' intensity and focus come at a cost. They can burn out their teams, depriving them of both the nurturing and sense of ownership that deepen their skills and form the basis for scaling the enterprise.

 ## The Explorer:
Curious, Systems-Centric, and Dispassionate

Builders who are Explorers are not necessarily motivated to build a new business from scratch, but they are inveterate problem seekers and solvers. Whether the problem is designing better pantyhose (Sara Blakely of Spanx) or unlocking the potential of e-commerce (Jeff Bezos at Amazon), their solutions may focus on product or process, or both. These men and women become stand-alone entrepreneurs or builders of new ventures inside existing corporations because building new businesses seems the best way to solve and commercialize their solutions.

Once hooked by the problem, they fixate on execution, at least until the next intriguing problem emerges in search of solution. Their management style is hands-on to the point of being overly controlling at times.

Explorers are systems thinkers who like to tinker with how a system works to develop a better approach. As a result, they tend to be quite empirical in their decision making, relying on the relevant facts and underlying logic of the issue, rather than emotion or intuition.

These builders attract similar problem solvers, who build their own confidence after demonstrating their particular systems-thinking chops. Explorers can be rather dismissive of areas in their companies that don't relate directly to their primary passion for solution design. For example, they may feel that sales and marketing are necessary nuisances (after all, their brilliant solutions should practically sell themselves).

 ## The Crusader:
Audacious, Mission-Inspired, and Compassionate

Crusaders are primarily motivated by an intense desire to make the world a better place—by solving problems that matter to markets and society. The crusade may be ice cream with Ben & Jerry's social mission, a designer dress made affordable for a special occasion by Jenny Fleiss and Jenn Hyman's Rent the Runway, or a more responsible approach to managing garbage, as it is for Nate Morris's Rubicon Global—the Uber of the waste management business. Anchored in a deep-seated ability to empathize with others, Crusaders create mission-based companies with bold, long-range vision.

They have a clear mission, and appreciate—indeed, even look forward to—the opportunity to invite others to help bring it to life. In that sense, Crusaders have an unusual mixture of both sensitivity and humility, combined with a confidence in their animating vision for their business. Unlike Explorers, their decision-making mode is highly intuitive and anchored in their almost instinctive sense of what is right.

Crusaders are guided by their founding mission; however, they can struggle with tough people issues. While they are quite effective in attracting dedicated followers inspired by the company's mission, they frequently avoid conflict, allowing devoted underperformers to languish rather than removing them from the business. On the operational side, Crusaders often find themselves out of their element and don't always provide the clear direction that other Builder Types do.

 The Captain:
Pragmatic, Team-Enabling, and Direct

Captains are as much team assemblers as catalysts. These builders are intent on creating a company culture around values and mutual accountability. Comfortable with leading from behind, they trust their colleagues and culture to fulfill the vision for the company whose future they share. Unlike Explorers and Drivers, they find gratification in the *we* rather than the *me*.

But these men and women are Captains nonetheless, with a clear notion of where they want the ship to go and what needs to be done to get there—although they are more willing than their three builder counterparts to hear ideas from others first. They are motivated to build enterprises of enduring value through unleashing the productive potential of the individuals and teams around them.

As leaders, Captains believe in setting clear goals and expectations, then delegating responsibility for execution. While they prefer consensus-rooted decisions, they sometimes manifest an iron fist in a velvet glove when their teams underperform.

Their decision-making style tends to be unemotional and focused on growth, while they are careful to be consistent with mission, vision, and prior personal commitments. Captains are arguably the most fully developed leaders in terms of direct, honest, and consistent communication among the individuals and teams they manage. But their more consensus-based approach can lead to a form of incrementalism that may miss the necessity or opportunity for more dramatic, disruptive innovation in their markets.

Which Builder Personality Is Most Similar to Yours?

While the descriptions you read on the preceding pages are the simplest way to identify which Builder Personality Type you are most like, here we will show you a bit more about how our typing process works.

The instrument appearing on the facing page represents a simplified version of our Builder Personality Discovery™ (BPD) quiz. For each ques-

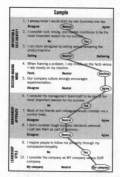

tion, we invite you to circle the response that best captures your view. You can then draw a line down through each answer, as shown in the sample to the left.

In Appendix B, we have plotted the response pattern for the archetype of each Builder Type so you can compare yours to each type and discern which is most like yours.

For this paper-and-pencil simulation, we have collapsed the potential answers for seven of the questions from a seven-point scale to three answers (disagree, neutral, and agree) to facilitate your ability to see the pattern that best matches your responses.

There is a reasonable amount of variation within and across questions for each Builder Type. As you would expect, the archetype for a given type does not capture this variation, so we strongly encourage you to visit our website at www.builtforgrowth.com. There, our algorithm converts your set of answers along the full seven-point scale to an accurate assessment of your type.

You may be wondering why an algorithm is needed. There are over one billion potential answer patterns to these questions, so this analysis is not the work of the traditional pencil-and-paper approach.

The Builder Personality Discovery Quiz: Find Your Closest Match

MOTIVATION & SELF-IDENTITY

1. I always knew I would start my own business one day.

   Disagree   **Neutral**   **Agree**

2. I consider luck, timing, and market conditions to be the most important reason for my success.

   No   **Yes**

3. I am more energized by selling versus delivering the product/service.

   Selling   **Neutral**   **Delivering**

DECISION-MAKING MODE

4. When framing a problem, I rely mostly on the facts versus I rely mostly on my intuition.

   Facts   **Neutral**   **Intuition**

5. Our company culture strongly encourages experimentation.

   Disagree   **Neutral**   **Agree**

MANAGEMENT APPROACH

6. I consider my management team/staff to be one of the most important reasons for my success.

   No   **Yes**

7. Most of my friends and colleagues would consider me a control freak.

   Disagree   **Neutral**   **Agree**

8. I don't consider tough business decisions personal. I just see them as part of business.

   Disagree   **Neutral**   **Agree**

LEADERSHIP STYLE

9. I inspire people to follow me primarily through my compassion/empathy.

   No   **Yes**

10. I consider the company as MY company versus OUR company.

    My company   **Neutral**   **Our company**

The Dynamic Challenges Every Business Builder Faces

In this book, you'll see how each of the four Builder Personalities handles the challenges and opportunities in creating long-lasting, large-scale business value for customers, investors, employees and themselves. Regardless of the setting in which the builders work, they all face a set of recurring dynamics that test their ability to succeed. Whichever Builder Personality you are, you are likely to encounter five dynamic challenges that stand above the rest. Each deals with transforming a particular resource or aspect of the business: its solution, team, customer, sponsor, and scale. We call them the *growth dynamics* (figure 1-1).

These five growth dynamics will both demonstrate and expose your personality's strengths and weaknesses. Some will be conquered easily; others will challenge you to your core.

We use the term *dynamics* for several reasons. These challenges continuously change, as the nature of the business, its stage of maturity, and industry setting vary. They also happen not necessarily sequentially but often simultaneously. And they recur throughout the business-building process. In the hands of the strongest builders, these dynamics can transform business value.

The term *growth dynamics* also captures the essence of what's involved in building a business. In broad usage, dynamics are defined as "the forces or properties that stimulate growth, development, or change within a system or process."[4] That is dead on. Physicists use the term to refer to the branch of mechanics concerned with the motion of bodies under the action of forces—also a pretty accurate, if analogous, description of what happens to emerging ventures as their builders struggle to survive and achieve scale.

This book focuses on the interplay between each Builder Personality (the who) and the five growth dynamics (the what). This interplay is where value is created, transformed, or destroyed.

FIGURE 1-1

The Five Growth Dynamics

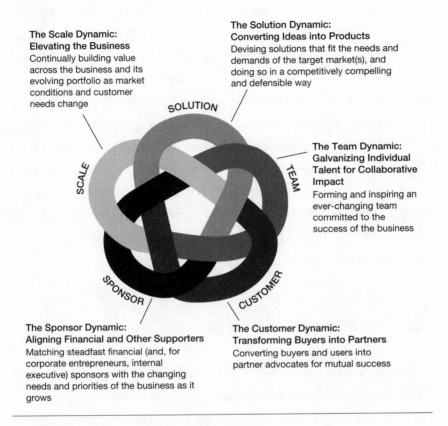

The Scale Dynamic:
Elevating the Business
Continually building value
across the business and its
evolving portfolio as market
conditions and customer
needs change

The Solution Dynamic:
Converting Ideas into Products
Devising solutions that fit the needs and
demands of the target market(s), and
doing so in a competitively compelling
and defensible way

The Team Dynamic:
Galvanizing Individual
Talent for Collaborative
Impact
Forming and inspiring an
ever-changing team
committed to the
success of the business

The Sponsor Dynamic:
Aligning Financial and Other Supporters
Matching steadfast financial (and, for
corporate entrepreneurs, internal
executive) sponsors with the changing
needs and priorities of the business as it
grows

The Customer Dynamic:
Transforming Buyers into Partners
Converting buyers and users into
partner advocates for mutual success

The Interplay of Who and What: How Builders Engage the Growth Dynamics

In these pages we do not simply define and describe the four Builder Personality Types. We look at these builders in action—how their behavior and preferences are reflected in why they are builders, how they make decisions, and how they manage and lead through the rigors of the key growth dynamics.

No single Builder Personality Type holds the key to success: each builder fashions his or her own blueprint for building. Some builders' strategies work better than others' strategies, reflecting the gifts and gaps of each Builder Type. But together, the strategies of all four types offer a portfolio of pragmatic lessons you can apply to leverage your own particular strengths, address the challenges your business faces, and—in the process—become a stronger builder.

With stories and examples drawn from our personal interviews and other sources, we will show you how each Builder Personality Type handles these challenges in many business settings. Regardless of your Builder Type, you can learn from each of the other three. Armed with these powerful insights, you can improve your own odds of building business success—whether you're in an independent startup, creating a new business within a larger corporation, considering starting a new business, or otherwise engaged in society's imperative agenda of new-venture creation.

How This Book Can Help You

We're not the first authors who seek to understand the phenomenon of building successful businesses from scratch or to understand personality, for that matter. You can find clues to such success in biographies of legendary entrepreneurs—from Andrew Carnegie, Henry Ford, and Larry Ellison to Mary Kay, Arianna Huffington, and Oprah Winfrey. These stories can be fascinating, educational, and even inspiring. You can learn much about what it takes to launch, grow, and sustain a business that way.

This is not a book about the mechanical steps of launching a startup or another venture, product-market fit, or the keys to innovation. Lots of other books do that. But great recipes don't make great restaurants—great chefs do. While each of these books can be useful, they miss the most important element: specifically, who the builder is and how his or her personality engages with the dynamic challenges every entrepreneur faces.

By understanding the gifts and gaps that go along with your Builder Personality, you can better tackle the fundamental challenges of business survival and growth to scale. We'll offer you practical suggestions for how you can become a stronger builder, using the patterns of success and failure of each personality in addressing the various growth dynamics.

Builders of new businesses work inside and outside existing corporations. In these pages, we examine both types of builders. The role

Work Our Research Is Based On

Our book is anchored on two foundational pillars, one in personality and one in business growth. The first is the decades-old tradition of personality research, which you may be familiar with through widely used instruments like the Myers-Briggs Type Indicator (MBTI), the DiSC Profile, and Hogan Assessments.[5] The second is Geoffrey Moore's classic work, *Crossing the Chasm*, which laid out the fundamental challenges companies face in scaling across five customer segments, from innovators and early adopters to early and late majority and, finally, to laggards.[6] Moore's work greatly influenced our thinking. In the same way he found that businesses encounter a different set of challenges across the different customer segments (an insight that led to the original Rosetta methodology), we show how leaders and founders encounter a different set of challenges across the core activities of launching and scaling a business.

that Builder Personality Type plays is similar no matter where a venture is being pursued. Along the way, we will, however, highlight some of the contextual nuances in different settings.

If you're thinking of becoming a builder, we can help you learn the patterns of success that lead to achieving scale. You can easily determine which Builder Personality is most like yours and how to benefit from your counterparts' hard-earned insights in handling the challenges ahead.

If you're already working in, or considering joining, a new venture team, we'll help you understand the builder at its center and figure out how to collaborate most effectively with his or her growth agenda. And if you're a funder or sponsor of new ventures, you'll see how to spot and support each Builder Personality to improve his or her odds of growing a business of meaningful scale.

We know from personal experience that change is difficult. So the advice you'll find in these pages will range from easier approaches that enhance your natural strengths to changes that are far more difficult because they may require confronting some of your deepest misgivings or even fears. You can then decide which strategy is right for you.

While building a new business from scratch can be intensely lonely, our message is you are not alone. You can take comfort and wisdom from those builders—famous or not—who share your Personality Type, and you can learn from them. Likewise, other Builder Personality Types can show you how they leverage their strengths and buffer their weaknesses—insights that may help you as well.

How *Built for Growth* Unfolds

In part 1, we profile the four Builder Types in detail, devoting one chapter to each. Through our personal interviews with extraordinary men and women who exemplify each Personality Type, we examine how their approach has enabled them to make their mark across the business landscape. We share the stories of well-known entrepreneurs like Ben Cohen and Jerry Greenfield (of ice cream fame) and Jack Dorsey of Twitter and Square, in addition to lesser-known founders like Nate Morris, Grace Choi, and Steve Breitman, who have built noteworthy value in their own endeavors—in sanitation, cosmetics, and apartment laundries, respectively. We include corporate entrepreneurs such as Chris Pinkham, the inventor of the underlying technology that enabled Amazon Web Services; the late Charlie Cawley, who built MBNA, the credit card behemoth, out of a small department within Maryland National Bank; and legends like Norbert Berta, who created the caplet dosage form that helped the Tylenol brand recovery from the notorious 1982 poisonings.

Using many of these examples, we illustrate how each Builder Type approaches the dynamic challenges at play in building a highly successful business—where does each create value, and where does each risk destroying it? What makes these men and women tick? How do they make decisions, manage, and lead to grow their businesses? We conclude each chapter with a blueprint offering practical advice you can put into action immediately to become a stronger builder by leveraging your innate strengths and buffering your weaknesses by delegating to others the activities that constitute your weaknesses.

In part 2, we pull the lens back from the Personality Types to examine three key kinds of crews builders must assemble to build for growth. In chapter 6, we examine the deeply personal decision of whether to join forces with a cofounder, and if so, which Builder Personality Type of collaborator may fit best with your Personality Type. Chapter 7 discusses how you can recruit a team that works best with you, and chapter 8 focuses on attracting the financial investors or executive sponsors that best match your Builder Personality.

Part 3 constitutes a single chapter. By this point in our book, you will have learned there is no single successful Builder Personality Type. Each builder can be successful in his or her own way. We suggest two strategies to becoming a stronger builder. With the first, the *expert builder* strategy, you concentrate on your talents—or, as we term it, elevate your gifts—and delegate the tasks and responsibilities that are not your strengths. With the more ambitious approach, which we call the *master builder* strategy, you borrow and adapt some of the gifts of the other Builder Types—making them your own through practice over time.

The path to becoming a master builder will challenge you to examine some of your longest-held assumptions and tendencies, both of which may stem from your deepest aspirations and apprehensions. In this final chapter, we arm you with the knowledge and practical steps to begin truly expanding your builder repertoire beyond the confines of your own Builder Personality. In so doing, you are not *becoming* another builder. Rather, like all master craftsmen or world-class athletes, you are learning strategies that work for your counterparts and—with effort—can be translated to work for you, too.

We welcome you to this journey of self-discovery. In the pages that follow you will likely see yourself or perhaps fellow builders you work with or are inspired by. Most importantly, we hope that as you close the final page, you will feel equipped to become a stronger builder for growth.

A Builder Personality Tour through Silicon Valley

Let's see these personalities in action by taking a quick spin through the heart of Silicon Valley. Take a look at how each Builder Personality has shaped the structure, growth trajectory, and culture of four iconic companies.[7]

Apple's Driver

Our first stop is on everybody's short list of startup-to-standout success stories. Leaving aside how revolutionary Apple 1.0 was in transforming the computer industry when Steve Wozniak and Steve Jobs got started, consider the stamp the prodigal Jobs himself left on this company after his return in 1997 to spearhead the stunning revival of the company. His personality—born to build, an intuitive decision maker, with a controlling and often abrasive management style—shaped that company's entire destiny. Jobs was a Driver's Driver—relentless in lashing his company to his singular vision of "insanely great products" he knew the world (and his customers) needed, even before they did. This kind of market-sensing capability, propelled by an obsessive drive to launch the perfect market-fitting product, typifies the Builder Personality we call the Driver.

Apple under Jobs's direction was not a "we're a big family" organization. It was—and is—a proud, defiant, and famously secretive place under the spotlight scrutiny of its brilliant, if sometimes mercurial, founder-CEO. Its fusion of beautiful design simplicity, functional technology, and innovative business models continues to reflect the transformative power a Driver can have—even when he or she sees way beyond everyone else's headlights.

Facebook's Explorer

In building Facebook into the global phenomenon it is today, Mark Zuckerberg revealed his Builder Type's defining curiosity, systems thinking, and fascination with an interesting challenge: how can I attract, engage with, profile, and then connect with my friends or people I'd like to date? Zuck, as his friends know him, epitomizes the Explorer personality.

Although Facebook's headquarters are just up the road from Apple's, you'd think you were in a different world altogether if you roamed the halls of Facebook and talked with its employees. Attracted by the fluid problem-solving atmosphere, people are encouraged to align themselves with projects that excite them. The workplace environment is filled with handwritten signs and team notes on almost any available surface. Facebook's chief people officer says: "We're intentionally trying to mold roles around people rather than people around roles. That puts people in a place where they can do their very best work."[8] Not exactly the kind of crew Jobs would have commanded.

Google's Crusaders

"Organize the world's information and make it universally accessible and useful"—it's hard to imagine a more ambitious initial company mission than that (except perhaps Google's other one: "Don't be evil"). But that's the crusade Google's cofounders, Larry Page and Sergey Brin, embarked on in 1998. Since then, Google has redefined how we use the web, redesigned concepts of the workplace, and refined its business model—separating its wildly successful advertising business from its "moon shot" initiatives like self-driving cars. The open, shoot-for-the-moon culture of Google and its parent company, Alphabet, reflects the comparably creative but looser management approach that characterizes the Crusader personality.

Both of Google's businesses are essentially search engines: one for what is, and the other for what might be. And each reflects the more accomodating style of their Crusaders, builders who are comfortable with a great deal of experimentation. Their Crusader visions are bold and broad.

HP's Captains

We end our tour where Silicon Valley arguably began, not far from the famous one-car garage where Bill Hewlett and Dave Packard launched their eponymous company with $568. They had a vision for not just their technology, but also for the kind of company they wanted to build. Their combination of technical wizardry and leadership wisdom put a distinctive stamp on their creation for more than half a century. Both Hewlett and Packard were Captains, builders focused not only on producing great products but also on creating a great team-based culture.

Their Captain personalities translated into what is commonly referred to as "the HP way."[9] It reinforced the importance of teamwork and acted as a guide to tough business decisions as well as an inspiration for what the company stood for in the hearts and minds of its people and its customers. Although HP has lost its own way in recent years, its history suggests a proud heritage that may be tapped again for future success.

Our Research Approach: Applying a Proven Methodology to Discover Builder Personality

We used the same proven, patented research methodology that one of us (Chris) and his team at Rosetta (the digital marketing and consulting firm he built) developed to decode how different consumer personalities operate in hundreds of markets around the world. Rosetta's Personality-Based Clustering technique has been used for nearly twenty years in service to leading companies in health care, consumer technology, financial services, and retail. Among its many clients were Johnson & Johnson, Bristol-Myers Squibb, Genentech, Capital One, Fidelity, Citibank, Microsoft, and Samsung.

The Rosetta research methodology answered a fundamental question: who buys what products and services, and why? For this book, we applied the same methodology to answer a question further upstream: who builds the businesses that sell those products and services in the first place, and why?

Whom We Focused On

Building a successful business and growing it to large scale is a marathon effort. We do not focus here on the general personality characteristics that might differentiate the runners of that race from the public at large—things like risk tolerance, comfort with ambiguity, ambition, a sense of independence, and personal initiative. You can read elsewhere about those traits that are shared by most entrepreneurs the world over, whether they are successful or not.

We concentrate instead on the winners of the marathon—the successful men and women who have built businesses that have survived and grown. These entrepreneurs are, and have, *built for growth*. Their companies have withstood the test of both time and market. Some of their enterprises are valued at over $100 billion, while others have annual revenues a small fraction of that. But virtually all of the entrepreneurial builders in our study have defied the odds in building businesses that have achieved longevity, impact, and scale that distinguishes them. While there is obviously no guarantee the builders we've selected and their ventures will survive indefinitely, they have nevertheless outlasted most other runners in this marathon.

How We Did It

Our first task was to discover the factors that separate builders into groups in which their motivations, beliefs, and preferences explicitly drive their approach to building for growth. We designed a quantitative, one-hundred-question survey instrument based on our combined experience as consultants, investors, and professors and on Rosetta's proven methodology for developing questions that isolate the personality dimensions that drive different behaviors. Next, we fielded the resulting survey to a national pool of successful entrepreneurs, builders of companies whose survival and scale have defied the odds.

Using Rosetta's methodology, we then analyzed billions of potential respondent-answer combinations to discover and ultimately profile the four distinctive Builder Types. Our algorithm looks at every combination of question and response to identify the smallest number of Builder Types so as to simultaneously maximize the similarities within each type and the differences between that type and all others, using the fewest number of questions. This method allows us to categorize successful builders into one of these four personality types, but also accommodates the occasional hybrid builder who, while predominantly one type, also shares characteristics from one or more of the others.

The factors that distinguish each Builder Personality from the others (motivation, decision-making mode, management and leadership approach) also provide the basis for what we call the polar complement of each type. We coined this seemingly contradictory term to signify the type who is the polar opposite on these defining factors, which in turn drives opposing preferences and thereby, behaviors. But, within each type's opposite lies both the mindset and corresponding skill from which the other type can learn, hence the opportunity for being one's complement.

This concept of accelerating one's personal growth through understanding and then accessing certain aspects of one's opposing preferences is based on the work of Isabel Briggs Myers and Katharine Briggs, which in turn drew upon Carl Jung's work on psychological types.[10] We explore these opportunities for cross-type learning in detail in chapter 9.

Our modeling also enabled us to distill the original instrument into the ten-question BPD quiz introduced earlier. We then administered the BPD to successful builders across a broad business landscape, from independent startups to internal new business initiatives. Thousands of successful builders have now taken this questionnaire.

To expand our understanding of each Personality Type, we conducted in-depth personal interviews with dozens of builders of each type. In addition, we reviewed published insights on other prominent successful entrepreneurs, many of whose stories you will read in these pages. (See Appendix A for additional explanation of our methodology.)

A Disclaimer

Since we explicitly studied successful entrepreneurs, this book does not attempt to explain the causal difference between the winners and losers of the marathon of building new businesses for growth. We believe more can be learned from them than the wannabes.

We designed this book as a practical resource for independent and corporate entrepreneurs, their teams, and sponsors. Our research seeks first to understand how Builder Personality shapes the growth path of the business and, second, to offer practical advice on how you can become a stronger builder.

We consider this book the beginning of a collaborative journey to understand the dynamic interplay between Builder Personality and the building process. Our research is exploratory and the insights it has revealed will no doubt be refined as others examine this critical intersection. We welcome that. Further, our advice to each Builder Personality is based on our own extensive work as consultants, investors, and professors, but it, too, is hardly the last word in explaining entrepreneurial success. Entrepreneurship is far too complex a phenomenon for that.

So we invite you as readers and others in the field to build on our initial research in mapping this intersection between Builder Personality and the growth dynamics of building great businesses. We hope as our ideas take hold, a body of new insights and advice will be developed and shared among builders and those who support their quest for growth.

Finally, for a more detailed explanation regarding the issues of accurately determining Builder Personality Types consistently and the question of hybrids of two or more Personality Types, please see Appendix A.

PART ONE

THE BUILDERS OF GROWTH

How Drivers, Explorers, Crusaders, and Captains Build Differently

I n this part of the book, we delve more deeply into the quartet of Business Builder Personalities, focusing on the particular strengths and weaknesses of each one. Each chapter will describe and illustrate the distinct personality of each Builder Type and how each one operates within the context of the five growth dynamics.

As you read the in-depth descriptions and stories in these chapters, pay attention to which Builder Personality Type seems most like you. Does the preliminary self-assessment you did in chapter 1 still feel right? Or do you think you identify more with another Builder Type? Maybe more than one of these chapters describes you. That's OK—many of our leaders and entrepreneurs identify mostly as one type, but over time develop strengths that are more associated with another type. In fact, in the later chapters of this book, we will show you how you can learn from all of the Builder Personalities and deliberately take on and practice some of their strengths as an explicit way to address some of your own particular weaknesses.

In addition to rich descriptions, the chapters in part 1 include specific suggestions for playing to your strengths, buffering your weaknesses, and developing strategies to become a stronger business builder.

We summarize these elements in an at-a-glance format at the end of each of these four chapters:

Chapter 2   **The Driver:**
Relentless, Commercially Focused, and Highly Confident

Chapter 3   **The Explorer:**
Curious, Systems-Centric, and Dispassionate

Chapter 4   **The Crusader:**
Audacious, Mission-Inspired, and Compassionate

Chapter 5   **The Captain:**
Pragmatic, Team-Enabling, and Direct

2

THE DRIVER

Relentless, Commercially Focused, and Highly Confident

If you buy my mussel-shell ashtray, Mrs. Teetor, you won't have to worry about ash getting ground into your rug.

—*Chris Kuenne, age seven, Driver and Rosetta's founder*

One of us (Chris) will share a bit of his own entrepreneurial story: I've been an inveterate marketer since I first got the idea of painting the mussel shells I found along the shores of Lake Champlain and selling them as ashtrays door-to-door on Thompson's Point, where generations of my family have spent summers. It was 1969, and I was seven years old.

I went up to Mrs. Teetor's house. She smoked like a chimney. I explained the benefits of my painted shells: she would never have to

The Driver Profile

Factor	Description
MOTIVATION	• Always saw himself or herself as an entrepreneur. Ignited by ideas, driven to commercialize them with a fervor that feeds a Driver's self-confidence.
DECISION-MAKING MODE	• Initially intuition-based, but then seeks data and other external points of reference to triangulate and refine decisions.
MANAGEMENT APPROACH	• Hands-on, directive, exacting with low or no tolerance for failure.
LEADERSHIP STYLE	• Results- and outcomes-focused, tends to attract and inspire like-minded perfectionists. Has a harder time with followers who are not equally driven and goal-oriented.

worry about ash getting ground into her rug. I also pointed out how nice they would look around her porch.

Next I went to Mrs. Colby's cottage. She didn't smoke, but I figured she would buy my ashtrays because she was very proper and grew up with my grandmother. My pitch to her was different. I suggested she needed ashtrays on her porch when she hosted guests who smoked, while also subtly playing to our multigenerational family connection.

From that point on, I realized I had the blessing some considered a curse: I am a commercial animal—or, as my dad used to put it, I had a dollar sign for a brain. Although at age seven, I would not have described this as an intuitive drive, it nevertheless was. I had a sense of what people wanted and the drive to make it and convince them to buy it.

Fast-forward twenty years. Working at Johnson & Johnson (J&J) on the Sesame Street Vitamins brand, I found a problem with the conventional approach to segmenting consumers. The approach lacked the personality insight I had intuitively used at Mrs. Teetor's and Mrs. Colby's doorsteps. My early customers, although of similar age and background, bought for two very different reasons.

In the spring of 1998, I dusted off my ashtray-selling skills, built a PowerPoint pitch, and sold Bristol-Myers Squibb and J&J on my idea for a better, more actionable way to segment customers to improve sales effectiveness. For each client, we discovered the target segment of consumers whose underlying preferences best aligned with each brand. This insight allowed marketing teams to adjust their pitch to each consumer target. We proved this practice made their marketing three times more effective than their prior approach. The results were like my earlier success with selling ashtrays door-to-door: with over-the-counter remedies, personality-based sales and marketing worked much better.

Over the succeeding thirteen years, my Rosetta team and I further refined and patented our Personality-Based Clustering approach to customer segmentation, embedding it in each major form of digital marketing—from building e-commerce sites to customer-relationship marketing. This methodology became the basis for scaling Rosetta to become the world's largest privately held digital-marketing company, before we sold it to the Publicis Groupe for a record price. In fact, Personality-Based Clustering is the same approach my coauthor and I used to identify the four Builder Types for this book.

In the parlance of Builder Personality, I am clearly a Driver. Early on, I discovered that my purpose was to identify market needs and commercially exploit them as a form of personal validation. If you're a Driver, you were born to be an entrepreneur. You're motivated to discover unmet customer needs through a market-sensing intuition and then propelled to build a superior solution, even at a young age. You're comfortable basing decisions on that blend of confidence and gut instinct.

As Drivers, we have a management approach that is very hands-on and intense, and we expect our colleagues to be equally fixated on impact. For me, this style proved effective early on in attracting many enormously talented team members whose gifts led to Rosetta's scale and success. However, my leadership style proved challenging as the company scaled to nearly a dozen offices and more than twelve hundred people. I fell into the trap of many Drivers who define themselves through tight control over everything, confusing the seductive quality of management control with genuine leadership—a Driver tendency we explore later in this chapter.

How Drivers Engage:
"I Know What Customers Are Looking For. Trust Me!"

If you're a Driver, you engage each growth dynamic with intensity and confidence. When it comes to the solution dynamic, you are in your element, sensing market direction and fitting your product to needs that customers may not yet even know they have. Your intense drive helps in recruiting expert employees, early-adopting customers, and certain investors who stoke your need for validation and market impact. But at successive levels of scale in which leadership requires releasing such a tight grip on every aspect of the business and empowering others, you begin to run into challenges. Let's take a look at each growth dynamic to understand the pattern.

The Solution Dynamic:
Converting Ideas into Products

Ben Weiss is the builder of Bai Brands, the wildly successful new-age beverage that has quickly gained distribution across the country—and, with it, brand loyalists. Weiss started his career in beverages by working on a coffee drink for Godiva Chocolates. This assignment led to his belief that coffee, and its source, the coffee bean, perhaps held the key to a totally new kind of drink. He began experimenting with the coffee bean's shell—the part usually discarded—because he knew it is actually rich in antioxidants.

Weiss sensed the diet and nondiet beverage segments had evolved to a point where a new opportunity was taking shape. As he explains, "The millennial consumer said, 'I don't want to drink my calories and I don't trust artificial sweeteners.' So, when I stumbled upon the formula for Bai (making it with a blend of natural sweeteners including stevia, so it only has five calories), I found the answer to the diet dilemma. It's the intersection of 'good for you' and 'great tasting.' We are the *Bevolution* and we're redefining flavor without sacrifice."[1]

If you're a Driver, your desire to plumb market need and develop product-market fit is a nearly primal instinct. Howard Lerman is a Driver and the builder of Yext, the leading location-based marketing firm. The firm is responsible for ensuring that more than 2.5 million small businesses have their street address, telephone number, and hours of operation accurately represented in every major search engine. Yext helps ensure consumers can move from an internet search to finding the physical store location. When we asked Howard about this challenge, he said: "Translating an idea into reality is something I specialize in. We saw early on that proper representation in Google, Yahoo, and Facebook was going to be fundamental for every business on the planet. But ideas are a dime a dozen. The thing I really do that sets me apart is, when I see something, I'll keep at it and actually make it happen. I have an intense bias for action."

The Driver has a unique combination of intuition and intensely focused discipline. While many people may tend to be either more logical or intuitive in their thinking patterns, Drivers have both tendencies. As a Driver, you are particularly focused on creating and capitalizing on customer value. You dismiss those who say luck plays a key role in business-building success. You believe your success is a function of your talents, and you deliberately focus these talents on an opportunity for which you sense the market need and address it through careful market experimentation, feedback, calculated risk-taking, and your innate selling abilities. Your Driver's confidence and ability to convince others of the value in your solution translates into the sales equivalent of "I win, you buy."

"If I analyze the situation . . . hold the problem . . . I can see the flow."

We observed this very same passion to identify and capitalize on product-market fit in the fashion industry. Mi Jong Lee is a fashion designer in New York City, selling her collection, Emmelle, through her own retail store as well as in more than sixty-five other stores throughout the country. Lee's compulsive market sensing has been one of the keys to her success.

She describes how she obsessively watches, studies, and thinks about the underlying needs and wants of her target customers, professional women ages forty to fifty-five: "I know what they want. It's the fit. It's the fabric. It's the aesthetics. I'm dressing women elegantly, but those women don't want to stand out. They can be feminine, sharp, but not too sexy."

Lee's drive to serve this professional woman is a delicate balance between intuition and facts. As she puts it, "I have to say it is mostly intuition, but I like analyzing. I am forever analyzing. This may sound strange, but I've always found that if I analyze a situation and I hold the problem and just observe, I almost can see the flow of where the market is going." This organic balance, propelled by a strong personal drive for commercial success, is reflected in how Lee continues to run and grow her company. She says, "I always feel that, for me, if I lose that organic sense, I'm losing the whole sense of why I have this company."

The solution dynamic taps the Driver's defining gift. As a Driver, you relish each part of the process: from the inspiration that comes from your ability to sense how the market will develop, to your drive and confidence to translate this insight into something real. In fact, the energy that flows from your success in this dynamic carries over to each of the other dynamics, at least in the early going. Sometimes your energy is positive and deployed constructively, while other times it can obscure signals coming from others, occasionally leading to the alienation of team members and sometimes even customers and financial sponsors.

You are likely to encounter this challenge at successive levels of scale as your initial product idea evolves to a portfolio of products or services and often from there to a genuine platform and the geographically distributed offices or divisions that come with it. Your desire to remain hands-on can work against your ambition to expand. You must empower others to build on and extend your initial idea not only to fit new and broader-ranging customer needs and markets, but also because with cocreation comes greater follower empowerment and thereby leverage. In other words, if you can let go of some of the creating, you will tap a reserve of creativity far greater than just your own in this dynamic.

Driver in Action

I was all over everybody every single day.
—Steve Breitman, SEBCO Laundry Systems

When Steve Breitman left the blighted Bronx neighborhood where he grew up, he swore he would provide a better life for the family he hoped to have someday. At the age of nineteen, he had saved enough money to purchase three coin-operated laundry machines. That was almost fifty years ago. He now owns more than forty thousand laundry machines (at $4 per wash, you do the math).

The Driver seeks hardworking followers cut from a similar cloth. Reflecting on the early days, Breitman says he "was looking for people who were willing to commit and put in as many hours a day as necessary and as much of their life as was needed." He describes how he trained people: "I worked side by side with people. It was like osmosis. They kind of started to live and breathe like me."

In terms of management style, Breitman says, "Twenty years ago, I was all over everybody every single day. I probably worked eighteen hours a day, six or seven days per week." This is the intensity of the Driver burning through.

While he was working all hours, Breitman also thought about how to build out the organization. He explains, "You need to align yourself with people who know the operational side, the finance side, and the marketing side of the business so you can put it all together. I was fortunate that I just have the skill in all of them myself."

The Team Dynamic:
Galvanizing Individual Talent for Collaborative Impact

Your market-sensing and product-creating energy also attracts some of the best talent in the early years of the company, when inventiveness is core to survival and initial growth. Howard Lerman was fortunate to meet his cofounders in high school.

Lerman has always been the ringleader. He describes how he saw opportunity and then inspired and directed his buddies in the early days: "When we started off, there were three of us in a little rowboat. Sean MacIsaac and Tom Dixon would row, and I would say, 'Row in that direction because I see something there.'" And indeed he did see something there.

From that metaphorical rowboat, Lerman and his high school pals created and sold Intwine, their first company, just three years after college. Intwine was a consulting firm specializing in Microsoft's .NET programming language. They grew Intwine to $5 million in sales, sold it to Daltran Media for $7 million, and then moved on to building their current venture, Yext.

Lerman now leads a company of nearly a thousand people, but continues to inspire through his market-sensing strength. As he puts it, "Now I'm CEO of an armada. There's a giant ship in the middle and twenty-eight smaller ships around it, and they all have complex interlocking parts. The core of my job is now to steer from the middle, but when we make up a new product, I literally jump right back into that rowboat. We now call this process 'jumping into the pirate ship.'"

Lerman shows how Drivers leverage their market-sensing and product-creating gifts directly in attracting, inspiring, and directing followers. Unlike corporate CEOs, Drivers do not hesitate to create the next product themselves. Fueled by market understanding and self-confidence born from their commercial track record, they inspire employees, customers, and investors to follow.

As a Driver, you are most effective in recruiting the first set of expert team members and inspiring them with your commercial sense. Your real test occurs at subsequent levels of scale, when you must empower others to invent. Lerman learned to adapt his leadership style and role so that his culture accepts and is perhaps even inspired when he jumps back into the pirate ship to create the next big idea.

Certain industries, such as those centered on technology, allow for this kind of inventiveness to be powered by the builder and a small team. In professional services businesses, it works less well because client service teams must be able to invent on the spot and the Driver can't be the sole engine of client problem solving. In these industries, the Driver's skills of recruiting, training, and inspiring others are rigorously tested.

"I defined personal success as . . . changing the game."

Laurie Spengler is a professional services Driver hybrid, who blends the mission-centered values of a Crusader with the high emotional quotient of the Captain as a guide to her approach to team building. Spengler built, scaled, and ultimately sold back to her management team a company called Central European Advisory Group, which specialized in advising entrepreneurial companies in Eastern and Central Europe on how best to raise outside growth capital.

Spengler clearly draws from the gene pool of the Driver: "Early on, I defined personal success as being the go-to adviser for entrepreneurs in Central and Eastern Europe . . . To meet that gap in the market and . . . to change the game." However, Spengler also understands the importance of building and bringing the team along: "It's one thing to be the entrepreneurial founder," she says. "The idea is super clear in your own head. You think to yourself, 'Wow, this is all so obvious.' But it's quite something else to have to articulate that to others and really build the best of teams."

In her first staff meeting, Spengler surprised her team of experts by not lecturing to them for an hour (the norm in Central Europe), but rather spoke for two minutes and then posed a question, asking each person to provide his or her own answer. Later, one of her team members said, "Laurie, you know everyone walked out of that meeting very upset. They thought it was very strange that a founder would ask a question and wondered if that meant you did not know the answer."

Spengler was operating against the social norms of the region and against the Builder Personality preference for a Driver. But she is aware of the inherent tension all Drivers need to consider: how best to strike the delicate balance between leading by example, teaching, and providing the opportunity for others to develop and hone their own inventiveness. She explains: "I wasn't saying, 'I'm the founder here—I created this really neat business model, and I expect you guys to execute my ideas.' I was telling them I expected them to debate and challenge. If you're not hashing it out inside the company by speaking your mind and debating, we're never going to be able to advise our clients effectively."

This is where Spengler was channeling her inner Captain, because she knows the most important part of forging a powerful team, after recruiting the right players, is trust. As she told us, "I was clear that creating that atmosphere of trust, of candor, intellectual rigor, and engagement [came from my] leading by example."

So as a Driver, you should be mindful of the balance Spengler highlights. Your determination and gift for converting ideas to products inspire others to join you. However, you must subjugate your urge to create to your need for the operating leverage that enables scale. Such leverage can only flow from teaching and empowering others to create in their own ways.

The Customer Dynamic:
Transforming Buyers into Partners

"Wearing the annual forecast around your neck: 6,058,921 cases of Bai Brands."

Ben Weiss genuflected toward a bottle of his five-calorie Bai drink and explained how he has earned a coveted position with his largest customer, the Dr Pepper Snapple Group (DPSG) distributor: "I have a product here that does the heavy lifting. I have such a confidence in it that allows me to fight for my consumers every day." In this case, Weiss is referring to the fight with his distributor for more shelf space in stores, a fight he is clearly winning. As a measure of Weiss's charisma and confidence in himself and his product, he is now the darling of the CEO of DPSG, a $6 billion publicly traded industry leader.

In fact, Weiss convinced the CEO to wear a set of Bai-branded dog tags emblazoned with the annual sales quota Weiss recently negotiated with him to deliver. This is vintage Driver—create a product that has such exquisite product-to-market fit you can convince the CEO of a giant company to wear your annual forecast for sales to his company around *his* neck: 6,058,921 (to be exact) cases of Bai. Perhaps the most remarkable part of this story is that Bai was less than 2 percent of the distributor's annual volume at that time. But the strength of the product and the charisma of the Builder inspire his customer, the distributor, to go all out in support of both.

"I've worked with twenty-two agency partners across our ecosystem. Not a single one has ever done what you just did."

For a Driver, the very best outcome you achieve with your customers is to dissolve the boundary between your company and your customer. When your cash register rings, so does your customer's. Rick Greenberg, the builder of the Kepler Group, describes such an example in his fast-growing digital marketing firm. Greenberg's team was at the end of the first of a two-day offsite meeting with his client, planning the following year's marketing strategy. As a wrap-up to the day, Greenberg asked a question: "How do you guys allocate your marketing spending by media channel?" His client answered that it was done ad hoc—everyone opined, they fought a bit, and then they landed on an allocation that was anything but empirically derived.

Greenberg was hooked. Rather than accepting the client's offer to join them for dinner that night, he and his team pulled an all-nighter, developing a model to answer the channel allocation question on a more empirical basis. After seeing their work the next morning, the client exclaimed, "I've worked with twenty-two agency partners across our ecosystem. Not a single one has ever done what you just did." Part obsession over client need, part motivation to delight the client, and mostly the Driver's goal to serve his client better than any of his competitors, Greenberg's approach—like that of other Drivers—was to apply his product-market fit skills to convert his customer to a partner.

Len Pagon, like Greenberg, founded his company Brulant, a digital systems integrator, with a similar passion to "quickly generate trust and credibility with our customers." One of Len's customer growth strategies centered on building a channel relationship with IBM, becoming the largest independent implementer of its WebSphere e-commerce platform. This led to winning client relationships with several *Fortune 500* companies in the eastern United States, including TRW, Eli Lilly, BP, and several others.

As a Driver, you are particularly effective in mastering this customer dynamic in the early stages of building your company. You tend to do so with the customer segments Geoffrey Moore calls the "innovators" and "early adopters" in his famous book, *Crossing the Chasm*. These customer segments actively seek as-yet-unproven solutions to problems before the rest of the market even sees them.

However, don't confuse early growth ignited by the early adopters with the broader appeal required for scalable success. You are particularly vulnerable to falling into Moore's chasm—the gap between the early market and the later, mainstream market—because you derive so much satisfaction from customers who "get it." Remember, early adopters typically represent less than 15 percent of the market. To cross the chasm, you must attract and partner with both the early and later buyers, who represent the lion's share of many markets.

The Sponsor Dynamic:
Aligning Financial and Other Supporters

Ben Weiss's passion and sales momentum won him early investors ranging from Bill Bradley, the former New Jersey senator and National Basketball Association star, to Ashton Kutcher, the actor.

When he was raising money from his first backers, he merely placed a bottle of Bai in front of each person, suggested they take a sip, and then began to rifle through the sales velocity data at his best retail stores: "We are outselling Honest Tea by five times here, and we are at the sales rate of Vitamin Water there. Oh, by the way, Vitamin Water sold to the Coca-Cola Company for $3.5 billion." (This line proved prescient, since Ben signed a deal in late 2016 to sell his company for $1.7 billion to his distributor customer, DPSG.)

Most financial sponsors obsess over the question of product-market fit, or in the entrepreneurial vernacular, "Do the dogs eat the dog food?" This question is home base for you if you're a Driver. You relish the opportunity to demonstrate your deep understanding of customer need and how your product or service meets that need. You capture the imagination and confidence of financial sponsors by leveraging your core commercialization strength. However, as experienced investor and partner at Venrock, Bob Kocher, pointed out, "Drivers can be harder to work with, because they have total conviction they're right and some of them can be less susceptible to new information and changing their views or listening to their teams."

If you are a Driver operating inside a corporation, the sponsor dynamic represents a trickier balance than it does for your startup counterparts. While a startup Driver must attract the right investors, he or she can choose from many (if the Driver is good and has created momentum in a hot domain). As a corporate Driver, however, you are stuck with the existing sponsors inside your firm. In this case, you must learn how to temper some of your impatience in order to translate your vision into their budgeting and investment priorities. If you can do that, you may unleash enormous impact over time through the budget you tap and corporate peers with whom you collaborate.

Many corporate Drivers may find it difficult to adapt to the slower-paced complexity of the typical corporate environment. Your very drive and need for autonomy may turn into impatience and frustration. If that sounds familiar, you might want to take a deep breath before you walk out the door. Why? You may be leaving behind access to many crucial resources your outside counterparts would die for—things like early funding, access to proven talent to build your initial team, and entrée to potential customers or suppliers.

Ask yourself whether you and your idea might be better off if you pushed for an agreement with your employer to build your business under your current company auspices. Take a look at open-innovation companies like P&G, Nike, 3M, GE, Cisco, and Microsoft—not to mention Shell, Walmart, and many others—for examples of how big companies are demonstrating greater flexibility to accommodating your kinds of initiatives, which serve both your ambition and the interests of the corporate shareholder.

What may differentiate you from your corporate peers is your willingness to assume more personal and professional risk, and this can be your trump card. So consider offering to shoulder some of your company's risk in exchange for a more lucrative upside beyond what you would probably receive as a regular employee. This risk might take the form of phantom stock in your new venture, a negotiated super bonus tied to the venture's performance, a spinout arrangement with possible buyback by your sponsoring company, or even an equity split up front.

If all else fails and you decide to launch your idea as an independent venture, consider two other suggestions. First, make very sure your exit is a clean one—with no appearance of your having misused company resources, access to information, or other valuable assets to develop your idea on the company's time or dime. And second, leave as diplomatically as you can. You never know when you may find yourself across the table from your former employer as a potential customer or acquirer of your new business.

The Scale Dynamic:
Elevating the Business

In many respects, the scale dynamic is the toughest one for Drivers, because many of the factors that drive their behaviors in the other dynamics collide here. As a Driver, you have an obsession with creating products with exquisite market fit, a penchant for doing everything yourself, and an expectation that everyone you hire is like you in terms of skills, drive, and passion. These tendencies can conflict with the kind of followers you need to attract in the later stages of scaling your business.

Drivers tend to recruit early followers in their own image—hard-charging, confident experts who can discern the beat of the market's music. In the later stages, when roles are more defined, Drivers are forced to hire followers more comfortable following specific instructions. In some cases, the pure drive to achieve significant scale becomes the catalyst for change. In other cases, the fiery Driver chafes upon discovering followers who do not fit his or her ideal profile. Let's look at an example.

Adam Jackson, the cobuilder of Doctor On Demand (a health tech startup recognized in Goldman Sachs's "Top 50 in Digital Health" in 2015), is a classic Driver. He grew up in Cleveland and quickly realized he was far more ambitious and driven than those around him. Moving to San Francisco right after college, Jackson taught himself to code. He served other founders until he found a big idea he felt would change the game in health care: video visits with doctors over smartphones for acute conditions like cold, flu, rashes, and urinary tract infections.

Jackson, Phil McGraw (the popular host of the *Dr. Phil* television talk show), and McGraw's son launched the business in 2012. The service is now available as a benefit to major corporations such as American Airlines, Comcast, and The Home Depot, as well as to the policyholders of health insurance companies like United Healthcare.

Jackson describes his managerial approach: "I rely on myself, and I take a lot of pride in being hands-on and detail-oriented." On the one hand, Drivers tend to be controlling perfectionists. On the other, they realize that to achieve the scale and impact they aspire to, they can't do it all alone. Jackson explains how he resolved this conflict: "I learned this lesson in two tranches. The first was realizing there are only a couple of people like Kobe Bryant or Michael Jordan who single-handedly create billions."

He describes the second tranche of learning: "I was criticized for this kind of controlling behavior. That was painful, but I made it as constructive as possible . . . Sometimes I have to remind myself, but once you get past that hurdle, you are free to go find people way better than you and feel really good about putting those people in place where they can outshine you in order to scale the business."

As a Driver, you tend to approach the scale dynamic the way you conquer markets, new-product ideas, and customers—with the brute force of your personality. However, when it comes to hiring a leader of operations for your venture, you may run into an obstacle.

Matt Blumberg, the founding builder of Return Path, a global platform company that enables safe and effective email marketing for companies around the world, saw this firsthand: "As the company gets bigger, we've been getting into the nitty gritty of operating details. I would say that many of the people I've run across for these roles are complete and total jerks, and a large number we hired couldn't handle working in an environment like ours and didn't work out."

In our experience, those with strong operational skills find it difficult to balance the dictates of customer needs with the practicalities of operational efficiency. These hard-nosed operating leaders often choose efficiency over delving into the subtleties of customer and market. Since an intuitive mastery of market demand defines the Driver, it is inherently challenging to find operational counterparts who fit.

Driver in Action

We love it when other people are distracted from growing. We are never distracted.
—Charlie Cawley, MBNA

After being let go from Beneficial Finance earlier in his career, Charlie Cawley had something to prove.[2] In 1982, his boss tapped him to run the credit card portfolio of Maryland National Bank in neighboring Baltimore. Under Cawley's driven, fastidious, and occasionally imperious leadership, a small business unit was converted into the publicly traded credit card giant known as MBNA.

Cawley moved the credit card operation north, across the border to Delaware, where interest rate regulations were more favorable to card issuers. From an abandoned A&P supermarket, he began to apply his Driver gifts. At the time, big banks like Citibank, Chase Manhattan Bank, along with nonbanks like American Express, dominated the credit card market. As a loyal alumnus of Georgetown University, he had the idea of linking a credit card to the alumni association, reasoning other alumni might like to carry a card that benefitted their alma mater.

With the commercial sense and force of will that characterize a Driver, Cawley solved two problems at once: he differentiated a commodity piece of plastic we all carry in our wallets, while generating a new method to raise endowment funds for his alma mater. This Driver created the affinity credit card, just like those you probably have in your wallet or purse right now.

Cawley believed the customer is always right and customer care is essential to building trust and loyalty. Cawley and his team quickly proved and then scaled this magic affinity marketing formula for both new customer acquisition and exquisite customer care.

In less than a decade, Cawley's division of Maryland National Bank was more valuable than all the other assets owned by its parent combined. In 1991, MBNA went public as an independent entity. When it was acquired by Bank of America in 2006, it had fifty million customers, thirty thousand employees, and $120 billion in loans.

If you are a Driver, it is when you are scaling your support functions that you must conquer your urge to hire in your own image and to maintain your firm grip on the wheel. This is when the best Drivers release their grip. You need to hire for specific skills and empower others to flourish. When engaged effectively, the scale dynamic can spur enormous personal and company growth, if you're willing to allow your ambition for achieving scale to neutralize your central tendency to do it all yourself.

The Driver's Gifts and Gaps

We've seen how Drivers have a keen commercial instinct, fueled by self-confidence and perhaps even a chip on their shoulder to prove something to the world. If you're a Driver, you live for that moment when you can combine your sense of where the market is heading and your inventive spark to create the next big idea.

Will Margiloff, the CEO of IgnitionOne, a marketing technology company, typifies this characteristic. He told us, "I'm not a coder, and I'm not a technologist. I see where the market eventually will go. We saw the biggest problem marketers would have is integrating all the disparate pieces of technology. We were the first ones to figure out the cloud idea."

Your confidence and intensity attract talented followers who begin to fill out your initial team. Your commercial skills win both customers and investors as you build up a head of steam in preparation for leaping across Geoffrey Moore's chasm. But watch out! What got you to this point will not get you across. You are likely to hit an unexpected barrier that can keep you from achieving the level of scale to which you aspire. Your intense energy and need to prove something to the world as a Driver can—pardon the pun—also drive away the very people you need to scale your business.

Here is a quick profile of your gifts and gaps:

- **A keen commercial sense:** We saw how Ben Weiss capitalized on the intersection of "good for you" and "great tasting" to create the new beverage juggernaut called Bai Brands. It was that same sense that still leads Howard Lerman to leap back into his "pirate ship" to shape the next big idea at Yext. Laurie Spengler was driven by the same force, following the fall of the Berlin Wall, as she saw the opportunity to help emerging entrepreneurs fuel their dreams by showing them how to raise investment capital.

- **A creative impulse that enables you to convert customer need to a product or service that fits:** Mi Jong Lee, the fashion designer, applies this impulse to serve professional women ages forty to fifty-five. Adam Jackson figured how to bring a doctor directly to the patient with an acute condition like the flu through video chat enabled by the expansion of mobile bandwidth and the broad adoption of smartphones.

- **The ferocious intensity to make your venture successful:** This uncompromising focus was reflected in Ben Weiss's negotiation with the CEO of Dr Pepper Snapple Group, to ensure his five-calorie beverage would gain coveted shelf space in grocery stores across the United States. Similarly, it was this force of will and belief in their ability to crack the code on marketing mix that led Rick Greenberg and his colleagues at the Kepler Group to work through the night for one client to demonstrate they could optimize their media mix.

- **A tendency to overcontrol and underforgive your people:** Throughout our entrepreneurial and consulting careers, we have seen Drivers whose need for perfection and unforgiving nature chased away the unique talent their drive and vision initially attracted. A boutique consulting firm we know was launched by a Driver who was a former McKinsey consultant. In the early years, his firm was neck-and-neck with others like Oliver & Wyman and Alvarez & Marsala, both of which are now more than ten times larger than his firm. This Driver could not let go, allowing his need for control to choke out the independence and inventiveness of others to contribute to the firm's success, thereby inhibiting it from ever achieving the scale and impact he had originally hoped for.

- **Vulnerability to product narcissism:** By connecting your self-identity to your product, you can miss subtle signals from the market and fail to pivot when the need to do so is indicated. You may fall too far or too long in love with your product or service baby. Product narcissism is the equivalent of the innovator's dilemma for start-ups and can lead some Drivers to be one-hit wonders.[3]

- **A tendency to overreach with investors and customers:** One of the Drivers we interviewed told us, "I will go to the end of the earth to get the money I need on the terms I deserve. I've told plenty of people on Sand Hill Road [the favored address for many Silicon Valley VCs] to f— off." Your early market momentum can lead to an arrogance with investors—arrogance that can push your own valuation expectation so far above market you may not get the funding you need to continue to realize your dream of scale. Likewise, as growth and scale require expanding your customer base from tolerant and inventive innovators and early adopters to later-stage customers, you may have a hard time putting up with customers who aren't as imaginative but who are far more demanding on pedestrian issues that may not inspire you.

So what can you do with this mixture? Some people start playing to their strengths, or as we call it, *elevate their gifts*; others decide to work around their weaknesses, or *delegate their gaps*, and others employ a combination of both. Whichever approach you choose, here are five concrete suggestions you can start applying today to become a stronger Driver.

"Elevate and Delegate" Strategies to Become a Stronger Driver

In this chapter, you've seen how the Driver's single-mindedness and self-confidence can lead to exciting commercial success. But while this obsession can generate early momentum, it also presents challenges later on. Let's take a look at how you might address those.

1. **Shift from product creator to market scout:** In the early days, you saw the opportunity and conceived the idea, and your team

helped you build it as you sold it to early customers. As you scale, you should become more of a scout in the market, utilizing your ability to sense where it's headed. If you identify and specify what the market will need next, your crew members, if hired and trained correctly (see below), can cocreate with you. This shift in your role provides you with leverage and them with the sense of ownership and shared inspiration for what your company is bringing to the market.

But that requires sharing, and we appreciate sharing does not come easily or naturally for most Drivers. Chances are, your ability to share your gift depends on how well your colleagues pay attention to often-subtle shifts in market dynamics and customer expectations. And that, in turn, depends on careful customer listening.

Bring along some of your talented up-and-comers to watch you in action. Talk with them about why you ask the questions you ask, why you are curious about certain issues and trends, and how you try to stay ahead of what others are doing—but make it a conversation, not a lecture. Be prepared to listen to their ideas and instincts. Expect key employees who attend industry conferences to share what they've learned and observed, with a specific agenda of identifying the possible implications of those findings on your company's current strategy. They are your fellow scouts; don't shoot them.

2. **Don't expect everyone on your core team to share your passion and intensity:** While it may be ego-gratifying to surround yourself with comparably obsessed professionals, such team members may not be necessary or even helpful to scaling your business. It's more important to hire functional experts who are strategically aligned with that task and then give them enough open

road to drive their own work. Chances are, they work in areas you may not be particularly keen on anyway, like finance, operations, and talent management. These leaders need a deep understanding of your market strategy and the ability to incorporate that strategy into their functions, but you must also let them feel ownership over how they do their jobs.

When we spoke with Matt Blumberg, he saw himself (as did our Builder Personality Discovery instrument) as a Driver, but he also noted he shared some of the tendencies of a Captain. This observation and Blumberg's characterization of his journey as a builder are instructive for those who aspire to become more enlightened Drivers as they seek to grow their businesses through others. Blumberg told us, "I would say sixteen years ago, I did not fully understand how to create a learning culture that empowers through delegation, but now halfway through the journey, I do. And in so doing, I can unleash the power in others." Blumberg now obsesses over cultural fit, rather than cloning himself, when he recruits talent to grow the company.

3. **Don't let your product narcissism lead to innovation complacency:** It's great to take pride in your product, but remember—its life span is probably shorter than your admiration for it. Ben Weiss says of his "Bai-lievers": "I have people here, you cut their veins and Sumatra Dragonfruit [a Bai flavor] comes out." While this may sound like product narcissism, Weiss goes on to say, "I have always felt that the next Bai is in someone else's basement. We're just leading the change." If you've really cracked the code in your marketplace, others will follow quickly and, if you're not careful, perhaps even out-innovate you. Don't let this happen!

Remember, your early success stemmed from your commercial sense. Now you must start relying on your team to continue to evolve your current product offerings to ensure they fit with emerging customer expectations and competitive realities.

Dan Raju, the cofounder of Tradier, a financial-technology innovator for investors, traders, and advisers, did just this early on by hiring as his firm's chief technology officer a professional who was skeptical whether Tradier's core business solution could be produced. This person's team literally tried to disprove the theory of the founders, on the assumption that if their own skepticism could be overcome, the firm might actually be on to something. That baptism of cold water has now led to a thriving, growing business that simplifies the trading process for active stock traders.

4. **Admit you may not be the best salesperson for every prospective customer:** Drivers are often great persuaders and salespeople, sometimes accompanied with an intense "I win, you buy" approach to customer interactions. But as the market matures and the selling process becomes more institutionalized, you are no longer selling to like-minded early adopters. The sales cycle elongates and becomes more bureaucratic. You may find this infuriating to the point of actually alienating some of these less-inspired or less-decisive prospects. Consider delegating selling during this part of the growth cycle. If you have hired and cultivated your team members well, your sales force will do a better job than you, freeing you up for scouting the next solution opportunity.

One of us (John) learned this lesson the hard way years ago when building a national health business newspaper venture with a cofounder. Industry executives and health-care providers quickly became avid readers of the newspaper, and having personally convinced several major firms to become charter advertisers directly, I assumed I could do the same with the next tier of targets. But many advertising budgets were closely guarded by ad agency media buyers reluctant to recommend new channels in our market. Most were young people who didn't really understand the complex changes reframing the health-care business.

So in meeting after meeting with these gatekeepers to our next-stage prospects, I tried to impress, educate, and convince them why our publication made sense for their clients—with precious little to show for my efforts in terms of ad buys. I would leave these sessions exasperated. On reflection, I think my confidence in our product came across as arrogance to many of these folks. Finally, I backed off and let my sales staff handle these calls without my founder's ego getting in the way, with noticeably superior results. The moral: sometimes Drivers win from the shoulders, by letting other players on the road.

5. **Watch your hubris-to-valuation gap with financial sponsors:** Remember, almost every venture hits a rough patch along the way. You want to align with the right investors, allowing them an attractive return for the risk they take and the value they help you create.

   Several Drivers we interviewed (who shall remain anonymous for obvious reasons) acknowledge they had unwittingly boxed themselves into a corner by being too aggressive in hyping the value of their business with investors. As one expresses it, "Now that we have closed the round, we need to grow the business to fill in behind the valuation our investors just gave us."

   Given how many other factors are uncertain or beyond your control in growing your business, an early valuation victory with investors can prove to be a Pyrrhic one, if you overreached and then underperform. In these cases, you might require a flat or down financing round to extend your runway. So try to resist the temptation of many Drivers to reach for more than your fair share of the chips on the table, and leave room to reward your investors commensurately with the risk they are taking on. And remember: all bubbles are filled with air; make sure it's mostly your actual results and realistic prospects, not your own hot air, that support your valuation as you grow.

These suggestions for how you can better frame your own game as a Driver are just that—possible ways for you to elevate your strengths and work around or delegate some of your weaknesses. In chapter 9, we encourage you to move beyond these initial steps and put yourself on a steeper growth trajectory. We call this path the master builder strategy, in which you take on some of the strengths of another Builder Type and make them your own.

The Driver's Blueprint

Profile

Factor	Description
MOTIVATION	• Always saw himself or herself as an entrepreneur. Ignited by ideas, driven to commercialize them with a fervor that feeds his or her self-confidence.
DECISION-MAKING MODE	• Initially intuition-based, but then seeks data and other external points of reference to triangulate and refine decisions.
MANAGEMENT APPROACH	• Hands-on, directive, exacting with low or no tolerance for failure.
LEADERSHIP STYLE	• Results- and outcomes-focused, tends to attract and inspire like-minded perfectionists. Has a harder time with followers who are not equally driven and goal-oriented.

GIFTS (Strengths)

- Uses combination of intuition and fact-based analysis to anticipate market trends before competitors.
- Tenacity, ambition, and clear focus minimize distractions.

GAPS (Weaknesses)

- Overidentification with product can lead to missing new market shifts.
- Impatience with customers who don't get appeal of your product.
- May struggle with empowering expanded team as company scales.

Strategies for Growth

Strengths and Weaknesses by Growth Dynamic

Solution: Converting Ideas into Products

+ Market-sensing
+ Product–market fit
− Product narcissism

Team: Galvanizing Individual Talent for Collaborative Impact

+ Attracts experts
− Overcontrolling and underforgiving
− Alignment challenges with less driven and market-sensing team members

Customer: Transforming Buyers into Partners

+ Superior solution
+ Passion and drive to solve customers' problems
− Impatience with less innovative customers

Sponsor: Aligning Financial and Other Supporters

+ Strong product–market fit
+ Excellent early customer references
− Hubris-to-enterprise valuation gap

Scale: Elevating the Business

+ Intense drive for success
− Difficulty with empowering others

How to Be a Stronger Builder

- Shift from product creator to market scout
- Don't expect everyone on your core team to share your passion and intensity
- Don't let your product narcissism lead to innovation complacency
- Admit you may not be the best salesperson for every prospective customer
- Watch your hubris-to-valuation gap with financial sponsors

3

THE EXPLORER

Curious, Systems-Centric, and Dispassionate

They looked at me like I was crazy because no one had ever framed the problem that way.

—*Brian O'Kelley, Explorer, AppNexus*

"This is horrible! I hate it! I can't believe I ever hired you!" This verbal assault from his boss at Right Media greeted Brian O'Kelley after O'Kelley's six weeks of hard work in building an internet ad-serving platform.[1]

While a Driver probably would have returned to his desk, packed his box, and quit, the Explorer is more likely to respond with a question, as O'Kelley did: "OK, so tell me again: What is the problem you're trying to solve?" A deeper inquiry into the problem hooked O'Kelley on its complexity.

The Explorer Profile

Factor	Description
MOTIVATION	• Sees entrepreneurship as a systematic way to commercialize and scale solutions to the knotty problems that he or she is most curious about.
DECISION-MAKING MODE	• Highly motivated and systematic. Believes that every problem should be broken down into its constituent parts and carefully analyzed and that the best decision will be identified.
MANAGEMENT APPROACH	• Hands-on and directive, and expects everyone to be as systematic and curious as he or she is.
LEADERSHIP STYLE	• Tends to attract similar systems thinkers and builds confidence in others after they have demonstrated systematic problem solving and deep knowledge. • Sees others' successful management of key areas as a source of freedom to spend time where he or she can be most valuable to the company's future.

He learned the CEO was trying to create a platform for serving banner ads that solved two problems at once. One problem was how to optimize the price of a banner ad when different advertisers value it on different dimensions: some on the basis of cost per thousand people reached, some according to cost per click, and still others according to cost per acquired customer. The second problem was how to protect the platform from bidder price manipulation.

This kind of complex problem attracts an Explorer like a hot fudge sundae attracts a kid with a sweet tooth. It is multifaceted, requires an understanding of dynamic systems across multiple domains, and, if solved, can change the game itself.

The incumbent solution for this problem had been developed and commercialized by a company called DoubleClick. It relied on enormous computing power to crank through hugely complex calculations to set the price for each banner ad. O'Kelley saw the problem differently. In college, he had learned how a distributed network of servers could enable a significant increase in computing power. And from his courses in econometrics, he discovered the price-setting power of auctions.

Putting those two insights together, he created a prototype for an entirely new system. He and the founder then met with a team of Israeli entrepreneurs to show them their idea: "They were trying to solve a really hard ad-network problem with technology. What I did was change the business problem to one focused on setting price dynamically. They looked at me like I was crazy, because no one had ever framed it in that way. All the engineers were jabbering and mad because they did not think of it. All the businesspeople were jabbering because they thought it was brilliant."

Brian O'Kelley is a classic Explorer. His motivation to build stems from a deep curiosity in the way systems operate. He maintains a disciplined tenacity to keep working a problem until he cracks it. His decision-making style is linear, rational, and fact-based; he believes the best way to solve a problem is to break it down into its constituent parts.

O'Kelley went on to apply these same skills to build and scale his own company, AppNexus, the largest ad-serving company in the world. If you're an Explorer like O'Kelley, your type is reflected in your management approach as well, where you tend to be hands-on with respect to the most important areas of your company. Explorers lead through attracting and inspiring those similar to themselves—curious, systematic, and analytically gifted.

How Explorers Engage:
"What System Is at Play Here?"

If you are an Explorer, you get your Builder Personality Type label from your twin drives of curiosity and confidence to seek and develop a better approach to solving commercially valuable problems. You consistently bring your detailed systems thinking to every part of your business. You did not necessarily set out to be an entrepreneur, but rather are always on the prowl for the next puzzle to solve, the next mystery to decode.

Bringing your systems thinking to each of the growth dynamics works well most of the time, particularly as you build through the first few levels of scale. Launching your first products, winning early customers, and attracting your first set of investors are all challenges that can play to your linear, fact-based, problem-solving skills. However, as the business scales, you—like your Driver cousin—must fight the urge to do everything on your own and quiet the voice in your head that says, "But I could do it better myself." In fact, Explorers tend to be even more controlling than Drivers. Let's dig into each of the five dynamics to see how this personality unfolds.

The Solution Dynamic:
Converting Ideas into Products

As an Explorer, you're interested in solving problems to drive impact, not just to explore and tinker as a form of intellectual satisfaction. So you understand the importance of prototyping and iterative refinements along the way to create a final product you can demonstrate to potential customers.

"There has to be a better way!"

Explorers have a keen power of observation, not so much of people, but of systems and processes. They are fascinated by thinking through why something operates the way it does, and they constantly wonder if there is a better way to achieve the intended outcome.

For instance, why pay exorbitant prices for hard-to-find cosmetic colors when all the colors in the world exist on the internet and you can download and print them on the substrate of a blush or lipstick? This was the question Grace Choi, the builder of Mink, a 3-D printing company that specializes in makeup, asked. Or the question posed by Sara Blakely, who invented Spanx: Why are pantyhose and shapers the way they are? Is there a better way? These questions led her to create a more effective solution to the traditional girdle by providing greater coverage in a material that was more comfortable. Blakely said, "This discovery allowed me to find my purpose, which was to help women."[2]

The Explorer is attracted first to the problem itself—ideally a thorny one worthy of his or her time and talents. Often this happens by chance, as it did when Tom Leighton was working at MIT down the hall from Tim Berners-Lee, the inventor of the World Wide Web. One day, Berners-Lee told Leighton he believed traffic congestion and volume could significantly limit the potential and growth of the web itself.

That casual conversation got Leighton and his graduate assistant, Danny Lewin, intrigued with how such a massive problem might be tackled. It took a combination of brilliant algorithms and an excellent team that persevered through initial customer skepticism. The result was the creation and rapid scaling of a company called Akamai, a $2 billion global enterprise that now delivers much of the world's web traffic behind the scenes.[3]

Most Explorers are not MIT professors, but if you are an Explorer, you share that puzzle-solving spirit of fearless curiosity. You're drawn into entrepreneurship motivated by the belief you will find a better way to solve the problem.

Explorers are inquisitive; they look at things from various angles and perspectives, whether that's the "God's-eye" view from above or from the microscopic level up. They often outflank traditional industry competitors by thinking four or five moves ahead.

"I thought, 'How can I make this highfalutin concept real?'"

Tom Phillips, of Dstillery is another Explorer who, like Brian O'Kelley, is playing the ad tech game. In Phillips's business, the problem that hooked the founders of his firm was the belief that paying for ads on a price-per-click basis was attributing value to the wrong metric. Phillips believed internet advertising should be measured in terms of how effectively it builds a brand's reputation.

Phillips joined the company in its infancy after the founders had developed a core concept around consumer affiliation. They believed if they could figure out which consumers were attracted to a given brand, they could use personal affiliations identified through social marketing platforms (Pinterest, Tumblr, etc.) to spot similar consumers. With this insight, they felt they could launch more-compelling digital campaigns to drive a brand's awareness, relevancy, and reputation. Phillips explains what attracted him to take over as CEO: "They had created this highfalutin concept, and I thought, 'How can I make this real?'"

This is classic Explorer. Fascinated by a complex system and drawn into the commercial opportunity forged by the question, Phillips asked himself how the company could make the concept real.

The second problem that attracted Phillips was determining how digital interactions create brand value. "The claim that my platform is producing conversion for you gets a lot of marketers' attention," he says, "even if it is measuring the wrong thing. Clicking on a banner ad is not building a brand. It's a bit like the rooster taking credit for the sun coming up."

Phillips goes on: "Companies that sell these cost-per-click campaigns are sales-driven. Their technology is OK. What they do is highly expedient, but is of limited value. Running campaigns that get credit is easy; running campaigns that build brands is hard." For the Explorer, translating ideas into solutions involves two key elements: it must both function as intended and create measureable value.

If you're an Explorer operating inside an established corporation, you have the advantage of a target-rich setting with a host of complex problems on which you can focus your systems thinking and analytical strengths. The key to a career as a business builder, or at least to many years of gratifying impact, is to ensure your domains of exploration are aligned with the corporation's strategic focus.

Some of the most successful corporate Explorers pursue what we call the *headlights strategy*, solving a problem in their company's strategic field of vision—something the firm has already identified as an important problem. That's the story of Norbert Berta, whom you will meet later in this chapter and who literally saved the J&J Tylenol brand. At the very least, you will build your internal "suite cred" with senior executives—credibility you might redeem in getting the funding and talent you need to explore, solve, commercialize, and scale a venture initiative more of your choosing.

Some corporate Explorers prefer to work in private, at least until they're satisfied they've come up with an elegant, effective solution worth sharing more broadly. If you are one of these Explorers, you could think of it as your own skunk works, maybe in your garage at home or in your off hours.

After some Explorers have run this problem-experiment-solution cycle several times, their self-confidence begins to swell, and they develop what some colleagues may perceive as a bit of an intellectual superiority complex. As an Explorer, you may think you can disaggregate almost any problem into its constituent parts and then discover a better way to address it. This belief often leads you to enjoy solving problems alone, which is how you often come up with your best ideas. This lone-wolf approach, though, brings up the questions of how effective are you at leading and managing teams at successive levels of scale.

The Team Dynamic:
Galvanizing Individual Talent for Collaborative Impact

While Drivers attract followers with their self-confidence and tenacious pursuit of the goal, Explorers often attract people who share their deep-seated curiosity. But teams sometimes need technicians more than thinkers when the business grows larger and more complex.

As Brian O'Kelley put it, in the early days of building AppNexus, "I didn't really know anything about the finance function, but I read books, tore apart the P&L statement, and mastered how it worked. I just couldn't imagine doing it any other way." When asked what propelled this desire to understand his company's finances at such a detailed level, O'Kelley said, "It's not because of the money. In fact, I really do not care about money. That is not interesting to me, but understanding how things work is." In short, the Explorer pursues a deeper level of understanding of systems in order to control them.

So how does a control freak recruit, cultivate, and ultimately inspire others to become part of the team? You start with like-minded people. O'Kelley recruited his first followers into AppNexus from Right Media, where he had first cracked a key piece of the ad tech code.

The measure of O'Kelley's persuasion skills was reflected in his separation agreement with his former firm. He was entitled to take one person in contravention of his nonsolicit restrictions. He selected his chief technology officer, who received a very generous counteroffer by Right Media if he stayed for just one year. Yet the promise of how O'Kelley's new firm would solve the very same problem was more enticing. In fact, one year later, on the day the employment restrictions expired for O'Kelley's other key protégés, they also came aboard.

What was it about O'Kelley and his Explorer curiosity that drew this group of former employees to follow him into his next venture? It was the allure of the problem this Explorer had set out to solve and the track record he had already started to build in solving and commercializing high-impact solutions.

If you are an Explorer, the very thing that attracts your early team can become a challenge as you begin to scale. "Brian, you know the first hundred employees you hired feel like an elite corps, but the other three hundred people who work at your company feel like they are not part of the elect." These words came from an organizational development consultant who spent time talking to people at AppNexus. Upon hearing this diagnosis, O'Kelley's cofounder rushed to the defense of the first one hundred—their loyalty and camaraderie were exactly what he wanted. However, O'Kelley, ever the systems thinker, immediately shifted his management tone to counter the perception that favored the initial hundred—exposing a difference of opinion that would ultimately result in the departure of this cofounder.

This response is vintage Explorer. Attract like-minded followers, lean heavily on a favorite group—until doing so stalls scalability. Then, invoke systems thinking to see the problem through the eyes of the new people, and shift to a more meritocratic view of all employees to recognize and reward their contributions and impact. Some may see

Explorer in Action

It was 1999, and I was trying to save the tech industry from a coming train wreck.
—Derek Lidow, iSuppli

After completing a successful career as CEO of the company his grandfather had founded, Derek Lidow listed five problems that intrigued him. If he could solve one of them at commercial scale, he might be able to launch his own company. Although fundamentally an Explorer, Lidow also has a bit of the Driver in him, in that he was motivated to demonstrate he could not only lead a company but, like his grandfather, build one as well.

As he shared his idea for addressing inefficiencies in the supply chain for electronic components, many people quickly saw its appeal. Given his reputation as a thoughtful leader and deep problem solver in silicon chip design and manufacturing, Lidow had no difficulty attracting talent to this juicy problem.

With experts in place and early demand for a better way to source parts in a fast-growing industry, Lidow told us, "iSuppli benefited from many unfair competitive advantages: my good reputation in the tech community, my direct knowledge of what was valuable yet not being done well in the market, and my personal financial ability to kick-start development." However, these things rarely align perfectly by chance. Rather, they are evidence of this Explorer's gifts of systematic problem solving, anchored in the confidence he can create a better way.

It was a call from the company's largest customer that galvanized iSuppli. Lidow remembers the customer's ultimatum: "Throw out all you have been working on and deliver one million Tantalum Capacitors next month! If you can't supply this product, we will blame the delay of our global launch on your firm." Using his systems thinking and coolheaded attitude, Lidow assembled his team and disaggregated the problem into its constituent parts. He then deployed his people around the globe to source and deliver the parts to each plant on time—a virtual miracle. But not beyond the reach of a gifted Explorer.

This against-all-odds accomplishment was the catalytic moment for iSuppli. It helped coalesce a group of experts into a team willing to follow Lidow through fire to conquer a vexing problem no one else could.

this response as the work of a coldhearted mechanic who sees people as cogs in the wheel. We see it as tackling the problem head-on and understanding the mechanism at play—applied equally to product, process, or people.

Look at how Tom Phillips has built and measures his team at Dstillery. He uses metrics and transparent communication, constantly providing feedback. In fact, everyone is rated and measured every quarter. He calls it the "purge tool." The tool is a rating from 0 to 100, with truly exceptional performance earning above 100. "We are honest with ourselves and with each other," Phillips says. "If you are not at one hundred, say, ninety, we are telling you it is fixable. If you are at an eighty, we are telling you to go." Transparent. Quantitative. Unambiguous.

"We had something our competitors did not—super-pumped-up employees."

Another Explorer, Mark Bonfigli, the founder of Dealer.com, applied this same kind of systems thinking to improve the human-touch elements of recruiting and culture in his company, allowing it to scale to more than a thousand employees and ultimately selling it to Dealer-Track for over $1 billion. In the early days, Bonfigli and his cofounders were working so hard they all became dangerously unhealthy. A former high school tennis star, Bonfigli gained over fifty pounds; one cofounder developed Crohn's disease, and the other had to have his gallbladder removed.

Bonfigli got religion. He created a corporate wellness initiative with an in-house 20,000-square-foot fitness area, complete with an indoor tennis court, fitness instructors, and even an on-site masseuse. He realized if he did not make his company culture more balanced across the mind, body, and spirit, he and his team might fail to achieve their goal of changing the game in digital marketing for car dealers.

Soon, his wellness-focused culture was attracting high-energy talent. Bonfigli then realized his engaged and energetic sales and customer care teams could be a competitive weapon in the marketplace. He explains: "We did have a few inventions that were sort of cool and separated us, but the reality was some of our competitors had a more robust solution. We had something they did not have—happy, enthusiastic, inspired, and super-pumped-up employees who were smiling on the other end of the phone." What started as a systematic way to ensure the health of his workforce turned into Dealer.com's competitive advantage.

As an Explorer, you are a magnet for like-minded problem solvers. You are clear, to the point of being blunt, in your communications and your expectations for your teams. As the business grows, you should continue to apply your systems thinking to issues of talent management and look for opportunities like the one Bonfigli found in converting an employee benefit into a competitive advantage. After all, your people really are your key differentiator in the long run.

The Customer Dynamic:
Transforming Buyers into Partners

As an Explorer, you focus on problems. You work closely with customers to deepen your understanding of their problem, its context, and each potential use case. Then you work with a nearly religious zeal to engineer a superior solution. You may actually believe this intense focus on solving customer problems obviates the need for sales and marketing. In fact, Explorers might have a certain disdain for selling, believing the best products sell themselves. One Explorer explains, "We don't really care about selling or pushing the product. We're just focused on improving it, and then the selling takes care of itself."

If you are an Explorer, you focus your innovation on a new and superior way to solve one of your customers' toughest problems—making you and your solution particularly attractive to Geoffrey Moore's early adopter segment. It is this kind of customer who sees the potential of your innovative solutions. These initial customers are relieved someone else is on their side trying to solve their problems in a new, imaginative, and thoughtful way.

A key question for Explorers in this regard is whether you have the patience to wait for these market-lagging customers before turning your curiosity to a new challenge in the marketplace. Or if you don't have the patience, can you surround yourself with colleagues who do, so the company can truly harvest the rewards from your early breakthrough efforts?

On the other hand, the Explorer who sees the system in people terms may be able to attract customers differently. Bonfigli and his cofounders at Dealer.com forged a more emotional form of customer engagement, which began to dissolve the boundary between their company and their buyers, the goal of every new venture as it scales.

"When we saw your Halloween party, our CEO was a hundred percent certain we would work well together."

One day in late October, the Dealer.com management team was pitching to one of the biggest dealers in the country. At one point during this tense meeting, Bonfigli's cofounder glanced out the internal window at a ruckus on the floor below, and his heart sank. He had forgotten it was the company's annual Halloween party, when everyone dresses up and prances around the floor in their costumes, some of which were pretty wild. He looked at Bonfigli, getting his attention and signaling with the universal gesture of a finger across the throat, "We're done for!" Both Bonfigli and his cofounder thought to themselves in agony, "There's no way the management team, who has just flown into Burlington from Charlotte early this morning, is going to take us seriously if they see that these dudes from Vermont allow this kind of wildness in their office."

Bonfigli felt as if they had lost the pitch before it really began. At one point, the noise level was so high that the visiting management team went to the window and looked down at the wild costumes and all the energy and excitement. Off-kilter and embarrassed, Bonfigli and his team attempted to close the meeting and hustle their guests off to the airport. Bonfigli explains, "About three hours later, I get a call from the chief marketing officer, and she said, 'We just touched down, and I just want to tell you we were blown away. We want to move forward with a contract. We weren't a hundred percent sure in the meeting, but when we saw your Halloween party, our CEO was one hundred percent certain we would work well together.'"

For Explorers, systems thinking can pay off with customers, even when the system in question is company culture and employee morale and health, not just another clever algorithm. Bonfigli connected his understanding of human motivation with something missing in the car-dealership world—being authentic, somewhat silly, and having fun. In so doing, he unleashed a deeper and more enduring level of customer relationship, inspiring them to become true partners.

The Sponsor Dynamic:
Aligning Financial and Other Supporters

For some sponsors, investing in the ventures of Explorers makes sense because of the engineering mindset from which these builders create and commercialize. This compatibility can provide a common vocabulary and perspective. Explorer-friendly investors value a systematic approach to identifying and solving economically valuable problems. Many investors, appreciating the ingenuity of what Explorers are trying to do, are motivated by the possibility of earning outsized returns by combining the brains of the Explorer with their money.

As an Explorer, you may see problems arise when you expect your investors to be as engaged in the problem as you are. One Explorer bitterly describes how his investors "thought they owned us because they invested enough to control twenty percent. They were the biggest pains in the ass . . . They didn't care about our solution, if we weren't sleeping, if our people were unhappy. All they cared about was maximizing their return."

As an Explorer, you want to feel intellectually, if not emotionally, connected to your investors. You'd like them to appreciate the problem

Explorer in Action

The Bezos commitment to innovation inspires a level of inventiveness that does not occur in other companies.
—*Chris Pinkham, Amazon Web Services*

Chris Pinkham had just convinced the higher-ups at Amazon to let him return to his native South Africa for the birth of his first child and to continue supporting his work on a project that would ultimately become AWS (Amazon Web Services).

Before this move, when he was working for Amazon in Seattle in 2003, his curiosity led him to wonder whether there was a way to create "an infrastructure service for the world." He thought about the underlying problem: "the cost of maintaining a reliable, scalable infrastructure in a traditional multi-datacenter model." As an Explorer, he wondered whether there was a way to connect a distributed set of servers that could be deployed on demand, for any business customer, with unbounded expandability.

But then, back in his home in South Africa, Pinkham and a like-minded engineer named Benjamin Black teamed up to write a white paper on their idea, which can be a particularly effective way for a corporate Explorer to obtain financial sponsorship within a large company. Jeff Bezos liked the idea and gave the green light to develop it further.

First, Pinkham recruited and inspired a small team of engineers to develop EC2, the underlying technology that now enables AWS. By 2005, Pinkham was granted permission to engage with customers.

When we asked Pinkham (who, by the way, refers to himself as a "situational" rather than serial entrepreneur) what he believed enabled him to explore and commercialize EC2, he told us, "The Bezos commitment to innovation inspires a level of inventiveness that does not occur in other companies."

Distance helped, too. Years later, Jesse Robbins, who oversaw Amazon's technology infrastructure at the time, was quoted as having said, "It might never have happened if they weren't so far away. I was horrified at the thought of the dirty, public Internet touching MY beautiful operations."[4]

By 2016, AWS, enabled by EC2, served more than a million businesses and generated nearly $8 billion in annual revenue.

your team is focused on—and respect the elegance of the engineering your team developed to crack it. You feel the same pride as a parent showing pictures of her or his children, fully expecting some form of fawning. When investors don't provide this affirmation, they miss an opportunity to deepen the connection with the builder and the opportunity to strengthen the all-important bond of trust.

Explorers can also have contrasting motivations with their investors. The ambivalence Explorers sometimes feel for the investor who did not care about the solution was echoed in our discussion with Brian O'Kelley. The CEO of AppNexus is focused on improving and expanding his platform and ensuring his company continues to innovate in the ever-changing landscape of ad tech. In a heated discussion with an investor about an issue that would affect the CEO's compensation, O'Kelley deflected the point by responding, "You know, I have no idea what my salary is, and frankly, I don't care."

Although the primary source of alignment between builders and investors is obviously financial reward, it may not work as directly or as expected for Explorers. If you are an Explorer, you should be clear with your investors about the nonfinancial elements that are important to you, because investors are likely to be unaware of the power these can play in forging deeper alignment and trust. So look for a venture partner who is as intrigued by systematic problem solving as you are. Perhaps you may even want to make sure he or she is a fellow Explorer. You will find additional guidance on the connection between Explorers and financial sponsors in chapter 8, where we examine this relationship more deeply.

If you are a corporate Explorer, finding a financial sponsor inside the company is a key step in advancing your vision. Some pursue the explicit pitch strategy to those who control the budget. Another approach that can work particularly well is the *bootleg strategy*. Here, the Explorer works behind the scenes building early proof of product-market fit and economic viability. This approach can be especially effective if you have at least the winking acquiescence of your boss and company culture. And if you're lucky enough to work in a company whose culture resembles that of 3M, Gore (the famous maker of the revolutionary Gore-Tex material and products), or Google, you may even enjoy explicit permission to work on this kind of project on company time, at least within certain limits.

The Scale Dynamic:
Elevating the Business

Brian Coester, the founder of CoesterVMS, a company that enhances and simplifies home appraisals for residential mortgage underwriting told us: "It's not just about the technology. It's about the people. But it's not just about the people; it's about the combination of technology, people, and understanding." Coester was describing the artful way he has built out and scaled his residential home-appraisal platform. In fact, the core value of his platform is allowing home appraisers to scale themselves by codifying and simplifying the appraisal process.

Like many other Explorers, Coester stumbled on this problem as a young child, when he would occasionally accompany his father on home appraisals for local mortgage banks. The young Coester noticed that while his father was examining a house for sale, he wrote extensive notes on various pages held together on a clipboard. His father would then spend hours researching comparable homes before writing up the appraisal.

After college, Brian Coester began to think about how a computer platform could simplify and scale the appraisal business. He realized there was incredibly valuable knowledge embedded in the heads of all of the old-time house appraisers—knowledge that could be encapsulated in a checklist. He then mapped this information and determined it could be recorded in a database.

By comparing the data for each house appraisal to such a database of comparable values for other houses, the system could ensure the information each appraiser was entering was within an appropriate range, given other houses in the neighborhood. This real-time data check improved accuracy, reduced follow-up questions, and enhanced the mortgage underwriting process.

"Every person's core functionality has to do with getting the company better."

When we asked Coester how he scaled his business, he explained that since follow-up calls were the most labor-intensive part of his service, the company had to focus on resolving customer issues the first time around: "We asked, 'What could someone possibly call about?' and

Explorer in Action

I don't think they can ever sell another product under that name. There may be an advertising person who thinks he can solve this, and [if so] I want to hire him . . . to turn our watercooler into a wine cooler.
—*Jerry Della Femina, Della Femina Travisano Partners, commenting on J&J's Tylenol crisis*

On September 29, 1982, seven people were murdered by someone who introduced cyanide into Tylenol capsules and then placed them back on the shelves at several pharmacies in the Chicago area. The murderer had opened the gelatin capsule that contained the active ingredient in Tylenol, acetaminophen, and replaced it with the lethal chemical.

The use of one of America's most trusted brands as a murder weapon struck fear in the entire nation and led many to believe the brand should be retired. But not Norbert Berta, a Hungarian émigré who was a senior engineer at McNeil Consumer Products, the division of Johnson & Johnson that manufactured and marketed Tylenol. Days after the poisoning, this corporate Explorer began to ponder whether the capsule dosage form could be reengineered to be tamper-proof (or, to use the term coined later, tamper-evident).

Over the subsequent few months, Berta tinkered at home in his kitchen with different approaches, trying to figure out how he could compress acetaminophen into a tablet in the shape of a capsule. After experimenting with many approaches, he figured it out and the caplet dosage form was born. Since the caplet was solid, it could not be tampered with as easily as opening a capsule.

Norbert and the Tylenol marketing team quickly brought prototypes to retailers like Walgreens and Ralphs supermarkets to get their input and to demonstrate that because this solid dosage form was safe, the Tylenol brand could go back on their shelves. Berta quickly garnered executive sponsorship for his idea through his credibility and track record, moving from prototype to manufacturing. Given the scale of the number of caplets that would have to be made (literally billions to replace the entire national retail inventory), the engineering challenge was not small.

With an attractive solution, strong retailer support, and executive sponsorship that reached up to the CEO, Tylenol was relaunched in caplet and tablet form in 1983. Thanks to both J&J's culture of corporate responsibility to do whatever is necessary to maintain consumer trust and the inventiveness of a corporate Explorer named Berta, the Tylenol brand remains a key part of America's medicine cabinet.

then reverse-engineered the underlying cause into our platform. Every person's core functionality has to do with getting the company better." He then proudly told us, "We used to have twenty people in the call center; now we have five."

At CoesterVMS, everyone is expected to be a problem solver, even when this expectation leads to converting one's role into something the computer can do, thereby eliminating one's job. Coester's choice of the term "core functionality" reveals a perspective some Explorers hold. People are cogs in the system, and their contribution is described as "functionality," rather than in the more humanistic terms a Crusader or Captain would use.

Coester demonstrates how Explorers like to tinker with the way a system works to identify new ways to accelerate growth. If you are an Explorer, you have a keen eye for which problems offer the opportunity to create and capture value through a systematic and inherently scalable process.

The Explorer's Gifts and Gaps

Throughout this chapter, we have seen how Explorers apply their systems thinking and deep curiosity to identify and then exploit commercial opportunities. As an Explorer, you have a powerful set of gifts and have figured out how to apply them to generate economic value. However, your exceedingly high need for control and its secondary effects can hinder you along the path to scale. Here is a brief summary of your gifts and gaps:

- **Curiosity and systems thinking:** As an Explorer, you are endowed with an extraordinary curiosity, which motivates you to plumb the depths of why things operate the way they do. We saw this curiosity lead Brian O'Kelley, Derek Lidow, and Brian Coester to wonder why the incumbent approaches to banner-ad serving on the internet, the electronics component supply business, and the house-appraisal business, respectively, operated as they did. These and other Explorers apply a systems-thinking approach to their curiosity to begin a catalytic process that asks why, moves on to "I think I have a better way," and culminates in building and commercializing it.

- **Ability to make it real and scalable:** Another gift that distinguishes Explorers is their ability to understand how a system works, convert this understanding into an idea, and make the idea a reality. We saw this gift in action with Tom Leighton, Tom Phillips, and Grace Choi, respectively, as they each tenaciously pursued their ideas for managing internet traffic congestion, brand building through affiliations identified in social marketing platforms, and creating printable makeup. Explorers are not satisfied with merely figuring out how something works; they don't stop until they have made it better and then applied their systematic thinking to scaling that better solution.

- **Ability to attract talent:** In many ways, an Explorer can become a bit of a folk hero among his or her community of people drawn to a specific kind of problem. Explorers use the question "Is there a better way?" as a magnet to attract enormously talented and like-minded systems thinkers. Earlier in this chapter, we saw Chris Pinkham and Mark Bonfigli each attract the talent who could build, respectively, the foundation for Amazon Web Services and one of the fastest-growing digital marketing firms for auto dealers. In some ways your articulation of the problem and perhaps the beginning of a vision on how to solve it create the same force of attraction that Crusaders enjoy (see chapter 4). This gift allows you to recruit the followers you need to take on successively larger and more complex problems.

- **Autocratic predisposition:** You probably already intimidate many of your employees with your demanding standard of understanding how everything works and the speed with which you move from thought to action. While these factors may give you confidence, they can stifle those around you, leading them to become mere extensions of your will rather than true colleagues who can contribute far more.

- **Tendency toward "smarter than thou" style with support functions:** Most people have neither the processing power of the CPU in your frontal cortex nor your intensity. This combination not only intimidates those around you, but can also alienate them. Early on, when you are forming your team, this challenge may be less likely to show up, because everyone who is drawn to you, the problem you're focused on, or your vision is likely to share your intensity and thinking style. However, as you begin to build for scale and you need more functionally focused team members in finance, operations, sales, and marketing, some fault lines may open up between you and some of your people.

- **Detached, bot-like, tendencies:** Robot, that is. No doubt, everyone who works for you is already blown away by how smart you are and how you can solve problems nobody else around you can. This formula is your comfort zone and can be the initiating force that allows you to launch your venture and win your first few customers. However, to grow your business and ultimately to become a better builder, you need to stray out of your comfort zone and show a bit more of your heart as well as your head in interacting with members of your building crew.

"Elevate and Delegate" Strategies to Become a Stronger Explorer

Each of us approaches the challenge of self-improvement differently. Some of us prefer to hone or elevate our strengths first, others opt to concentrate on fixing perceived weaknesses, and still others choose an almost à la carte approach across their own mix of strengths and weaknesses, depending on circumstances or their sense of momentum. Whichever game plan you adopt, here are six suggestions to improve your effectiveness as an Explorer:

1. **Delegate more and sooner:** You're a solutions maven, not an operations expert. You should delegate a good deal of the day-to-day management of the company to others. However, in our experience, this is far easier said than done, because one of the core characteristics of Explorers is a strong need for control. If you are an Explorer, this need translates into your very hands-on approach with almost everything. Many of you build trust with someone else only after you are convinced the person has developed a deep and structural understanding of the domain equal to your own. This requirement can be a pretty high bar before you are comfortable loosening your grip and turning over the reins of a functional area such as finance, operations, or sales to someone else.

   We have seen some Explorers make this change from hands-on to delegator through the route of mentoring and teaching. As discussed, you are a gifted recruiter of talent. Mentoring that talent is the next step. In fact, you can satisfy your urge to control by showing others how you think, solve problems, and convert ideas to systematic action. You will find that many of the people you have attracted are already receptive to your approach. So give them the coaching they need to achieve the level of proficiency you require to let go. As your business reaches scale, the return on your efforts will be far higher in tackling progressively bigger and more complex problems, while building your crew members' capacity to operate the day-to-day business operations.

2. **Focus on next-generation solutions and beyond:** With your newfound time (from executing the advice above), you should stoke your

problem-solving powers by raising your company's solution set to the next level. This means converting stand-alone solutions to product or service lines, converting lines to platforms, and transforming the platforms to a plan for geographic market expansion. This kind of solution architecture at each level is likely to appeal to your systematic problem structuring and solving, while expanding the reach and impact of your venture.

This step, and step 1, requires you to let others in to your most private thoughts about where you feel your industry is headed. As an Explorer, you need insights and perspectives from others. And equally important, you need sparring partners to test and advance these ideas. You must fight your instinct to tackle this as a lone wolf.

As your business scales and the problems accelerate in size and complexity, you need to anneal your ideas in the heat of ideas of others who are your intellectual peers. If you have formed your board effectively, you will find some of this talent within that group, but also look in places like universities, consulting firms, and other industry thought leaders.

3. **See the system aspects in the softer issues:** Sure, it's easier to think through inanimate problems that have a consistent pattern to them, like machines and software. But it is the animate ones that actually scale and deliver your business vision. As Mark Bonfigli illustrated, you can use your systems thinking to address how best to attract, measure, and continue to cultivate the talent you need to scale. Think of it this way: your organization's culture may well be the most important code you crack to help your business grow to its full potential.

4. **Share the ball:** On issues large and small, you will create more ownership and, most importantly, a stronger emotional bond

between individuals and their work if you share key decisions that affect the day-to-day performance of your team. Ajay Goyal runs a fast-growing payments company called Prepay Nation. He is a classic Explorer who figured out how to use the cell-phone-billing infrastructure to transfer cash to family members around the world. He describes how he elevates the performance of his team: "We give our employees the freedom to work from home within the confines of clearly defined targets and objectives."

This strategy has attracted many working mothers who are diligent and committed members of his team, albeit from home. Ajay told us, "We don't have a heavy-handed approach. We give them the freedom, and they return the favor by going out of their way to make our organization run better." However, to ensure everyone is collaborating on a common agenda, he now asks each person to come to the office twice a week (or as needed) for white-boarding sessions. "We share ideas, problems, and identify ways to run the business better, from cost savings to customer service—we unleash the creativity of the group."

5. **Delegate to C-level buffers:** Consider relying on a highly effective chief people officer and a cadre of direct reports who can buffer the rougher edges of your intensity with your crew members. For example, Brian O'Kelley has several direct reports who do this for him, and Brian Coester has someone he refers to as "the adult in the room." This person helps translate his idiosyncratic style into less intimidating and more productive approaches others can follow.

For this delegation strategy to work, you'll need to select your lieutenants carefully. Ideally, they appreciate not only your rational problem-solving strengths, but also your vision, and, with the patience and tact you may lack or may be unwilling to invoke, they can help translate your vision to others.

6. **Show a little humanity:** Bryan Roberts, a venture capital partner at Venrock, has helped create many unicorns (startups valued at over $1 billion) in health care. He notes: "As people become more successful and important in the world, they become less like sentient beings and more convinced that whatever they do is right." Roberts's observation seems particularly important for Explorers, who have a tendency to distance themselves from others. In our experience, Goyal's approach of allowing his followers to get closer emotionally can engender a whole new level of awe and, consequently, inspiration. We encourage you Explorers to study carefully how Crusaders work their magic in this regard. A little emotional connection can go a long way for you.

Once you gain perspective and insight about which Builder Personality elements are holding you back, you can unleash a whole new set of strategies for growth. We encourage you to read all the chapters in part 1, because embedded in each chapter are lessons or techniques you can use to become a stronger builder. In chapter 9, we introduce the concept of the master builder and invite you to aspire to a higher level of building skills and techniques.

The Explorer's Blueprint

Profile

Factor	Description
MOTIVATION	• Sees entrepreneurship as a systematic way to commercialize and scale solutions to the knotty problems that he or she is most curious about.
DECISION-MAKING MODE	• Highly motivated and systematic. Believes that every problem should be broken down into its constituent parts and carefully analyzed, and the best decision will be identified.
MANAGEMENT APPROACH	• Hands-on and directive, and expects everyone to be as systematic and curious as he or she is.
LEADERSHIP STYLE	• Tends to attract similar systems thinkers and builds confidence in others after they have demonstrated systematic problem solving and deep knowledge. • Sees others' successful management of key areas as a source of freedom to spend time where he or she can be most valuable to the company's future.

GIFTS (Strengths)

- Systems thinking and analytics.
- Scaling on the systems side can be easier.
- Focused on constant improvement and solving the next problem.

GAPS (Weaknesses)

- Scaling on the people side may be problematic, especially in functions outside your interest.
- Sometimes brusque, impatient style can create morale problems.
- Can get sucked into solving less strategically significant problems.

Strategies for Growth

Strengths and Weaknesses by Growth Dynamic

Solution: Converting Ideas into Products

+ Is curious and a systems thinker
+ Develops breakthrough solutions to important problems
− Can lose interest after cracking the code

Team: Galvanizing Individual Talent for Collaborative Impact

+ Attracts expert talent
− Can be autocratic and impersonal
− Can be too tough on team members

Customer: Transforming Buyers into Partners

+ Solves complex and commercially important problems
− Can become impatient with less sophisticated customers

Sponsor: Aligning Financial and Other Supporters

+ Looks for systematic fit and is rigorous
− Has difficulty achieving alignment on nonfinancial issues

Scale: Elevating the Business

+ Focuses on systematic approaches
− Has difficulty emotionally inspiring and engaging a broad team

How to Be a Stronger Builder

- Delegate more and sooner
- Focus on next-generation solutions and beyond
- See the system aspects in the softer issues
- Share the ball
- Delegate to C-level buffers
- Show a little more humanity

4

THE CRUSADER

Audacious, Mission-Inspired, and Compassionate

I just felt that moms might want what I wanted—safe products for their babies, kids, and homes.

—Jessica Alba, Crusader, the Honest Company

An actress and former model, Jessica Alba knows the importance of healthy home products on a very personal level.[1] She has had asthma all her life and spent much of her childhood in and out of hospitals with various illnesses. When she was pregnant, she broke out in a rash after testing a baby detergent while getting ready for her first child. After researching other baby and home products, she realized how difficult it was to find nontoxic household products. This insight led to a different kind of birth four years later: the creation of the Honest Company, "a trustworthy lifestyle brand that touches everything in the home, that's nontoxic, affordable and convenient."

The Crusader Profile

Factor	Description
MOTIVATION	• To solve problems that matter to society, a marketplace, or both. • Driven from a deep-seated ability to empathize with others, feeling their needs and wants, and motivated to address them by creating a mission-based company.
DECISION-MAKING MODE	• Highly intuitive and driven from an emotional sense of what is right.
MANAGEMENT APPROACH	• Guided by their founding mission and intuition, Crusaders can struggle with tough people issues, as they eschew conflict and often allow underperformers to languish rather than be ushered out of the business.
LEADERSHIP STYLE	• Attracts talent to handle the more operational aspects of the business, inspiring them with vision and company mission, but not always directing them in a systematic manner.

Like many Crusaders, Alba identifies directly with the customers who need her products and are served by her business model: busy mothers trying to juggle hectic lives, raising kids, and wanting to buy healthy products for their children and homes. Her initial "aha!" discovery was realizing there was no single source or home-delivery service for healthy and safe products. This insight led to a search her husband described as compulsive. She was motivated to figure out a solution, talking with people, testing products, tinkering with various business ideas—all the while encountering skepticism.

"At first, people pretty much expected nothing from me," she explains. "I had nothing to lose—an attitude I took from acting and applied to business, trusting my gut. Trusting my gut is something I underestimated in business." Underestimated or not, Alba now presides over a venture focused on healthy environments that late in 2016 was in talks to sell to Unilever, the global consumer products company, for well over $1 billion.

While clearly ambitious and accomplished, Alba never saw herself as an entrepreneur: "I'm not a businessperson. I'm terrible at math." She's a big-vision dreamer, but also practical and frugal, a legacy of her modest upbringing—despite her more glamorous life since.

Crusaders are primarily motivated by an intense desire to make the world a better place by solving problems that matter to markets and society. Building a company happens to be a good way to make both happen. This audacity is what provides Crusaders their magic and gives them their name in our builder quartet.

Derek Newell, CEO of Jiff, an enterprise health benefits platform, described his motivation to become an entrepreneur. He told us, "I always wanted to have a really positive impact on the world and decided that government and nonprofits were too slow, and the fastest way to get it done and to have a positive impact on people's lives was through building a for-profit enterprise."

Crusaders make virtually all of their most important decisions through the lens of the originating mission of their business. This approach can be invigorating to some, but frustrating to others, who are looking for clearer and more consistent guidance from the person in charge. If you are a Crusader, one of your challenges in building for growth is translating your mission into a level of operational detail others can follow. Let's look at how these factors play out for Crusaders as they progress through the dynamics of building and scaling a business.

How Crusaders Engage:
"Keep Your Eyes on the Prize!"

If you're a Crusader, you are the polar complement of your micromanaging cousin, the Explorer. You will recall from chapter 1, we coined this term to signify the type who is your polar opposite on most of the factors that define you as a builder and drive the differences in your behaviors. But their strengths act as counterpoints to some of your weaknesses. Crusaders believe in laying out a broad mission and then trusting their teams to know what to do. They feel this laissez-faire approach to managing is key to preserving a spirit of creativity in their organizations.

Many Crusaders did not see themselves becoming entrepreneurs per se. Some find themselves creating, running, and growing a company somewhat by accident, while others believe luck or perhaps even some divine intervention was involved. Regardless of how they became builders, Crusaders started companies as an effective platform to achieve the positive impact they seek.

Crusaders are very good at attracting passionate early customers, who are motivated by the mission and charisma this type of builder brings to the selling process. These builders appreciate—indeed, even look forward to—the opportunity to collaborate with others in bringing their vision to life. In that sense, Crusaders bring an unusual mixture of both sensitivity and humility. Early followers feel like they, too, are truly joining a crusade or at least a company with a clear purpose and vision. This sense of a mission imbues their work with meaning and, often, their lives with purpose. Likewise, the best of a Crusader's early customers are not just buying a product or service, but rather helping to fuel a new and better way to address an important problem.

If you are a Crusader, your challenges lie in operationalizing the mission-centered business at scale. The business trajectories of some

Crusader in Action

What if you could share your status with all your friends easily, so they know what you're doing?
—*Jack Dorsey, Twitter*

"just setting up my twttr." This was Jack Dorsey's inaugural tweet. He had just leaped across three centuries with his follow-up to Alexander Graham Bell's famous quote unveiling the telephone: "Mr. Watson. Come here!"

An inveterate inventor and software programmer, Dorsey grew up in St. Louis, where from an early age, he set out to change the world.[2] When he was fifteen, he built a more efficient taxicab dispatch algorithm, which in some ways was a precursor to Twitter's ability to connect people with one another.

In 2006, Dorsey sketched out a simple idea, nicknamed Status, to help his friends stay connected. Twitter cofounder Biz Stone says, "He came to us with this idea: 'What if you could share your status with all your friends, so they know what you're doing?'" Dorsey built the first Twitter prototype in two weeks and then launched it.

"He's a great guy, a great friend, a fun boss, but he's in over his head," remembers one of Twitter's early employees, reflecting on Dorsey. Others reminisce about Dorsey leaving the office early to go to yoga and dressmaking classes. Most recall the frightening day when somebody finally realized Twitter's entire source code and database had no backups.

Perhaps there is a message beyond the poetic justice in the name Dorsey first gave to the company that became the multibillion-dollar enterprise we now know as Twitter. The original name for the firm was Obvious.

Crusaders show the limitations of a more improvisational (though still intentional) management style when scaling requires standard operating procedures and systems. Ben & Jerry's typified this predicament when the company grew from $100 million to $200 million in four years, but added no additional profit to the business. At that scale, managing a complex supply chain drives the ice cream business—regardless of the flavor of the founders' social mission.

Let's look deeper into how Crusaders deal with the opportunities and perils of each growth dynamic.

The Solution Dynamic:
Converting Ideas into Products

Crusaders are big-picture people, although as we've seen in Dorsey's case, the big picture sometimes emerges from a small discovery. However the mission is born, the grand vision, often stated in beguilingly simple terms, can pose difficulties when it comes to translating the idea into terms less-visionary parties can understand or have the patience to actually make and deliver in the marketplace.

There's a bit of self-selection going on here. If you're a Crusader, you are probably quite good at finding kindred souls as potential team members, investors, and customers—people who share your appetite for the next big thing. It can be as simple as offering people free ice cream to prove yours is better-tasting than anyone else's. Finding the right people can be an inspiring, exciting journey. That very inspiration, rather than a demonstration or prototype (as the Driver or Explorer might offer), is the magic ingredient behind Crusaders' success with the solution dynamic.

"Landfills are the next cigarette."

While some entrepreneurs start in garages, Nate Morris began his crusade from a garbage dump.[3] After graduating from Princeton with a master's degree in public administration, he stumbled on the perverse incentive of the garbage-hauling business. The two largest players in the space, Waste Management and Republic Industries, generate much of their profits through owning landfills and charging customers a tipping fee for dumping each ton of garbage into the earth. With such financial incentives, Morris worried how the industry would ever be motivated to divert more garbage into the recycle stream.

Righting the wrongs of the waste business became his mission and that of the company he founded and runs, Rubicon Global. He created what is known as an *asset-light business*, in which his firm owns no trucks or landfills, but rather provides a brokering system, as Uber does with passenger cars. Morris aspired to help large customers like Wegmans Food Markets and Walmart divert more of their garbage to recycling. His company studied the contents of their dumpsters and bid out contracts to haulers who specialized in each kind of material—one hauler would take the glass, another the cardboard, and so on. In so doing, Morris figured out a way to increase the proportion of dumpster waste that could be diverted to recycling; his firm now often reduces the annual costs of his customers' garbage collecting expense by 20 to 30 percent.

Morris's recruiting efforts in his fledgling business were aided when Oakleaf, the first company to attempt this strategy, was scooped up by the industry leader. This powerful incumbent disassembled Oakleaf, leaving the vision of increased recycling as one more idea thwarted by the power of capital and the seduction of trading mission for money.

But this is the very stage on which Crusaders love to play. The vision was validated, the first company to pioneer this approach had been acquired by the "black hats" (in the vernacular of a classic western movie) and now the Crusaders must only ride in on their steeds, gallantly restate the vision, and draw the experienced talent to their side of the battle. And this is just what Morris did. Once their noncompete clauses had expired, Morris recruited the top five executives from the remnants of Oakleaf, attracting them with his mission and the opportunity to realize their original dream. Morris captured his motivation for the Rubicon crusade in the simple line: "Landfills are the next cigarette." Maybe soon, thanks to Morris and his business, Americans will have landfill-free communities like we now have smoke-free offices.

As Geoffrey Moore would describe it in *Crossing the Chasm*, Crusaders excel at securing support from early adopters willing to take a chance on a largely unproven solution to an important problem. These customers like to be in on the ground floor of helping build a big dream. The transformative value Crusaders can create in the solution dynamic is precisely the ability to attract newcomers—team recruits, early investors and alpha-stage customers—to the vision itself.

Capturing the "lost boys" through in-game advertising

Katherine Hays, a serial entrepreneurial leader, was the first person to build a new media business at scale capable of delivering the "lost boys" demographic of eighteen- to twenty-four-year-old men, who in the early 2000s had dramatically reduced the number of hours they watched television. She transformed a small tool company that served video-game developers into a major media company by figuring out how to insert what appeared to be outdoor advertising in the context of video games in real time. Massive Inc., her in-game advertising company, enabled major brand advertisers like Sprite and Dunkin' Donuts to show their ads as billboards in car-racing and first-person shooter games. This idea enhanced the perceived reality of the game while tapping an incredibly valuable audience.

Hays created something from nothing in the complex video-game ecosystem by aligning the interests of three constituencies. Most people might not see inserting advertising in video games as a crusade as worthy as diverting more garbage from landfills into the recycling stream. However, her approach reveals a key attribute of the Crusader: the ability to observe alignment gaps and opportunities in the complex network of interconnected players. She listened carefully to the wants and needs of game publishers, advertisers, and hard-core gamers and then stitched together a solution that created and captured enormous value. For game publishers, Hays helped to produce about 33 percent more profit per game sold. For advertisers, she delivered a highly valuable and difficult-to-reach audience. For gamers, she enhanced the immersive experience, making the games more realistic with current advertising campaigns that were simultaneously running in other media channels. Microsoft marveled at her creation and acquired her company for $280 million.

If you are a corporate Crusader, you face particular challenges inside established companies, unless your particular vision aligns clearly with the professed strategic priorities and competitive positioning of your firm. If it does, you can become an influential banner carrier, showing your colleagues—through personal example and leadership style—how to accomplish the company's version of the crusade you and the company care about. This kind of crusade is like any new product—it faces tough odds and needs lots of trial-and-error testing and the ensuing flexibility on your part to incorporate critical feedback into your planning.

If, on the other hand, your vision is not on your company's radar screen at all, be prepared for a different kind of campaign altogether. This situation calls for clever and creative translation that clearly connects your notion with something else your company does care about, whether that's differentiating your firm's brand reputation, getting on the Best Workplaces list, or winning the Baldrige Award for quality.

If you are a Crusader operating in either the corporate or startup context, converting your idea to product requires your missionary zeal to align the interests of heretofore-disconnected parties. Ben & Jerry's did it by connecting the best-tasting ice cream in the world to social activism. Nate Morris did it through leveraging technology to connect independent recycling haulers to national customers like Walmart. Katherine Hays did it by inserting advertising in video games in real time, making the game more realistic for gamers, delivering a valuable audience to advertisers and more profit to game publishers.

The Team Dynamic:
Galvanizing Individual Talent for Collaborative Impact

For Crusaders, recruiting inspired team members is a natural strength. Since your management style as a Crusader is to stay above the fray and remain focused on the mission, you rely heavily on your teams' competency in pursuing that vision. You must use your compelling vision to attract experts in the major disciplines of marketing, sales, research and development, operations, and finance—experts who share your passion for the mission and want to bring their own A-game to that endeavor. The most successful Crusaders develop the skill to identify the two elements of fit they require: functional expertise and passion for their mission.

However, the allure of the Crusader's cause can draw in followers by the appeal of the mission rather than through the hard competencies required to build and scale the enterprise. Crusaders' passion for their mission may obscure their less-than-stellar abilities to manage the daily aspects of the business. Some Crusaders assume they can avoid this problem by hiring their loyal friends. In our experience, doing so may actually exacerbate the challenge, creating a tension between empathy and execution.

That's what Angelo Pizzagalli, the cofounder of PC Construction, now one of the nation's two hundred largest construction firms, discovered. He's truly a builder's builder. He and his brothers, Remo and Jim, wanted a friendly, comfortable workplace to reflect their own relationship. It was an early element of a culture that came to be called the "PC way," but it had some downsides. "We had kind of a philosophy," Pizzagalli says, "We hired people we liked . . . 'Don't hire anybody you don't want to have breakfast with.' That sounds good, but our hardest thing was we didn't set the bar high enough for people. So half of those people turned out to be awesome, and the other half were everywhere from competent to not so good. And it took us forever to make the decision to fire them, because we liked everybody we hired . . . We were too tolerant." Too much focus on simpatico may pose difficulties for Crusaders—especially for those whose empathy outweighs their expectations for excellent execution.

"I'm successful at giving a lot of rope, but not too much."

A digital media company founded by Katherine Hays, who also built the aforementioned startup that inserts real advertising in video games, helps consumers create branded content they can share virally. At ViVoom, Hays seems to have struck just the right balance of attracting capable collaborators who thrive within a nondictatorial environment.

She explains her approach with her collaborators: "I try to make sure the team has a really clear mission so people can make their own decisions at every level. If everyone understands why we're doing it and what we're trying to accomplish, we will create better outcomes."

Hays notes who her best followers tend to be: "Someone who's not at the peak of his or her capability. Someone who, if only given an opportunity and some headroom and a little guidance, can grow significantly in their career, can leapfrog four or five places . . . I think I'm successful at giving a lot of rope, but not too much rope—doling it out at the right time so they're always just a little bit uncomfortable and have a little more to take on."

If you are a Crusader, you are probably good at attracting passionate followers, but those followers need your passion translated into nuts-and-bolts priorities, a practice that is not always a strong suit for your Builder Personality Type. If you struggle with this challenge, perhaps Hays is a good role model for you. She is very deliberate in linking mission to task, hiring those who have the competency, and then providing just enough room to grow.

As the business grows, your challenge as a Crusader lies in keeping your troops motivated over the long haul. In the early days of Ben & Jerry's, explain cofounders Ben Cohen and Jerry Greenfield, it was not uncommon for employees to come in on weekends with their own tools to make sure everything was all set for the next day's opening. Cohen says, "There was an energy and a feeling for all of us, working together and an excitement about growing something out of nothing." Greenfield adds, "They managed the business through the philosophy of 'If it's not fun, why do it?'" Cohen and Greenfield also pointed out that an "inexorable drift toward the mainstream" can easily compromise the very mission, vision, and values with which they started.

A final challenge for Crusaders arises from colleagues' tendency to see the builder as the personification of the mission itself—a view the builder himself or herself might also share. This impression can be a powerful magnet. But if you are a Crusader, it can also set you up for a feet-of-clay fall if your behavior or judgment do not live up to the ideals or values expected of someone carrying your banner. Your shortcoming can leave colleagues disillusioned and can open the door to the kind of cynicism that might corrode the inspired camaraderie of a Crusader-led business.

The meteoric rise and stumbles of Elizabeth Holmes, the Crusader who dropped out of Stanford University to found Theranos, is a case in point. Fueled by a self-confident, audacious vision of transforming health care (making early disease prevention a reality through access to action- able health information), the company began with a provocative idea for doing blood testing. Holmes attracted not only a cadre of dedicated, pas- sionate followers (including one of her former Stanford professors) to her team but a blue-ribbon board of directors to boot—not to mention an excited group of eager venture capitalists who signed up for the ride.

On the way up to a $9 billion–plus valuation in less than thirteen years, almost everything seemed fine to Holmes's band of disciples. But starting with some disturbing questions about the veracity of the company's sci- entific claims and then investigations by various regulatory agencies, her flaws as a visionary Crusader were revealed. Following multiple investi- gations by the Department of Justice and the Securities and Exchange Commission, in addition to numerous patient and investor lawsuits, many estimate Theranos to be worth close to zero as of the close of 2016.

As a Crusader, you sometimes need to keep in mind that vision is no substitute for supervision. Like all four types, a Crusader is like a Shakespearean tragic hero, in whose greatest strength lie the seeds of his or her downfall. So it is with some Crusaders in this team dynamic. A mission can attract many people with good intentions, but opera- tional competence aligned with the mission—a far more difficult task— trips up many of your fellow Crusaders as they try to achieve scale.

The Customer Dynamic:
Transforming Buyers into Partners

As a Crusader, you are more likely to struggle with the challenge of Moore's chasm (the gap between early adopters and later customers) than some other builders are. You are probably a great evangelist for your mission, and your enthusiasm and charismatic personality can persuade early-stage customers to sign on. The appeal of your mission and the values that accompany it can create a strong brand and help drive sales. The process is something more akin to recruiting. When you sell a new customer, you have more in mind; you are actually forging a partnership with this new buyer.

"We'll figure out a way to make it happen."

Nate Morris describes how he approached one of his early and then-biggest sales pitches. He was calling on Wegmans, the Rochester-based grocer and one of the mostly widely respected companies in America: "I walked in wearing khakis and a button-down shirt, no jacket. I was sitting in the waiting room, and there were four salespeople from Waste Management, all in suits and ties, formally dressed, very buttoned up, and I was more casual. It was very intimidating."

Morris entered the big boardroom with notes he had jotted down on a single piece of paper—the three things he felt he could deliver to Wegmans. But more important than the content of his pitch was who he was and how he connected with this potential first, giant customer. When the Wegmans folks called him back to tell him he had won the business, they told him: "It was a no-brainer for us. Your approach made us feel like we were part of your family, and you seemed to fit right into the Wegmans culture. There was no pretension. You were very humble; you stated what you wanted to accomplish. Your competitors were just a bunch of . . . sales pitches."

Morris reflected back on that meeting when he spoke with us. "I think we were coming from a very thoughtful place of integrity and a place that we wanted to showcase value."

The Wegmans relationship has been transformational for Morris's Rubicon because it led to securing Walmart as a client and, from there, many other major national players. For Rubicon, Wegmans had become the referenceable account every chasm-crossing entrepreneur dreams of. As Morris puts it, "They've truly been evangelists for our business. They like the fact they helped build our business and have been able to see it grow. They feel very aligned with our approach and our values and the way we look at the world." Wegmans is an archetypal example of the early adopter customer.

That's the kind of bond a Crusader can forge with a very early customer, even one that is on everyone's A-list of sales targets. As a Crusader, you can rely on the power of your vision to pull others to your agenda, rather than using the product-push approach often favored by your Driver cousins.

Jim Hornthal, a venture investor and serial builder with more than ten startups to his credit across a broad swath of products and markets, has used this ability well. He is somewhat of a composite, with a Crusader-esque sense of mission for his ventures, combined with a Driver's curiosity and confident market-sensing willingness to bet on his pattern recognition insights about emerging technology or social trends. And more recently, he's honed an Explorer-like fascination with cracking the code of complex systems, in this case applying the lean startup framework of rigorous, iterative hypothesis-testing with customers to "evidence-based" entrepreneurship and innovation itself. As he says, "The entrepreneur who is not willing to fire the hypothesis leaves no choice but to fire themselves."

The Sponsor Dynamic:
Aligning Financial and Other Supporters

Crusaders may struggle in their search for the right investors because their ventures are often ahead of the current perceived market. Building a new venture in this context requires patient capital willing to wait longer for financial returns.

Crusaders tend not to be motivated by power or control, but rather by a mission to fundamentally change the status quo, whether that's an industry pattern, a business model, technology, or even the world itself. As their name suggests, Crusaders are in it for the long haul. They are seldom looking for a quick payoff or cash-out, given the magnitude and difficulty of the mission they are pursuing.

For example, Katherine Hays has enjoyed solid investor support for her ventures so far, but has not developed the same level of bonding she has had with her team and customers. For her, the entrepreneur–investor relationship has remained more transactional—mutually beneficial but not necessarily deeply rooted yet.

James Currier is a serial entrepreneur who has started companies ranging from gaming to digital health and is now the managing partner of NFX Guild, an invitation-only accelerator. With all that experience, James told us "Now when I start a company, I don't take a dime. I know the game. If you take the money, you gotta exit. Make sure you want this because it's like a prison sentence. You take money from people? You have to exit from that. Until you exit, it consumes your life."

The good news for Crusaders is they tend to find their best funders through a self-selecting process in which both Crusader and funder seek the other for a common set of reasons. As a Crusader, you need patient capital that is fully bought into the mission and the inevitable ups and downs of the crusade that lies ahead. Likewise, experienced funders who see mission as a key element of their investment thesis are both attractive to, and good at attracting, the Crusader.

As mentioned earlier in the book, Jenny Fleiss and Jenn Hyman founded the breakout startup, Rent the Runway. Their company rents designer fashion outfits for about $150—outfits that retail for well over $1,000. Fleiss found an ideal investor in Scott Friend at Bain Capital. She describes their relationship like this: "I speak to him three times a week . . . and that's six years in. It was probably two calls a day with me in the beginning. You know, that's pretty cool and pretty special. He's gone above and beyond, and it stands out as a defining part of our experience."

Christina Seelye, the serial entrepreneur and builder of Maximum Games, doesn't look for purely financial investors: "I've always only really got strategic investors, the kind . . . that would . . . benefit in two ways instead of just financially." She looks for funding from other businesses whose own core objectives will be advanced by the success of hers.

Nate Morris attracted like-minded investors to join his crusade in the form of Leonardo DiCaprio, Henry Kravis, and Peter Kellner, managing partner of Richmond Global and cofounder of Endeavor, the global nonprofit that spawns entrepreneurial ecosystems around the world. Elizabeth Holmes did the same with her investors and high-profile Theranos board members like Henry Kissinger. In seeking well-matched funders, Crusaders sometimes return with their holy grail; other times, they come back empty-handed. But in all cases, a shared sense of mission, timing, and path are critical to Crusaders' success.

The Scale Dynamic:
Elevating the Business

In this dynamic, Crusaders must evolve their connections with employees—connections that in the early days were based on deep personal relationships. As a Crusader, you can have real difficulty moving away from such relationships, because it requires you to operate against your Builder Type. Here, you must move to a more systematic and de-personalized method of connecting with larger groups of employees, many of whom you probably do not know by name. This evolution begins when the company reaches about 100 to 150 employees or when it grows beyond a single location.

Jenny Fleiss explains: "Since we've grown so fast, our culture has changed. Inevitably, we have many more processes than we used to. I do not know everyone's first name. That said, I think Jenn and I still are a huge part of the culture. Our personalities created the values we put in place when we were thirty people. Back then, we identified ten things we thought were reflective of our company's culture. A lot of them are the skills we bring to the business. Some-times, it frustrates the hell out of me that it takes longer to get things done, but mobilizing a bigger team necessitates increased processes and coordination."

Christina Seelye would agree. "I'm real good at starting stuff and growing it up [but] I'm not the right person when it gets big and process-y . . . I would have to get dressed up!" She continues, "I'm a big-picture-you-work-it-out kind of manager," much like many of her fellow Crusaders. But she's lucky, because she tempers that mission-centric preference with a firsthand feel for the importance of customized customer service and logistics, having grown up learn-ing from her dad's work as a teamster in the warehouse business.

If you're lucky, you will find complementary colleagues whose pas-sion for operations matches yours for the mission ahead, or vice versa. That's been one of the secrets behind Fleiss and Hyman, who first met as students at Harvard Business School. Fleiss is the operational maven, and Hyman the imaginative marketing genius. The fact they share the same first name is just coincidental, though it's emblematic of their symbiotic founding partnership.

"You gotta look beyond the recipe . . . have imagination."

Angelo Pizzagalli ran into some problems scaling his construction business, first because his aversion to outside funding and leverage translated into pressure on current cash flow. In his words, "We *had* to make money!" That meant scaling was a job-by-job grind, and the growth opportunities from future investment in people, technology, or equipment were constrained by the profits available from the current portfolio of projects.

Pizzagalli found that reigniting the entrepreneurial spark in his key people was difficult as the company grew to become a major player in its industry and became more systematic and regimented: "We used to have a lot of discussions with some of the managers because they weren't acting entrepreneurially. Some of those were hard talks, you know, because we didn't want them to always follow the recipe. You never get a surprise if you just do that. You gotta look beyond the recipe . . . have imagination." In other words, as their businesses scale, Crusaders still want their companies to reflect some of the spark and spunk they themselves brought to bear in the beginning.

A challenge all builders face in scaling their companies is the tendency to hire people like themselves. If you're a Crusader, you may be especially prone to this hiring practice, given your emphasis on the inspirational vision that motivates you. This kind of doubling down on new hires who resemble the founding builders' own style may work up to a point. For example, Jenny Fleiss commented: "I think I have hired most successfully when I've hired mini-me's. I'm able to relate to most of those individuals—smart, type-A doers, self-starters, go-getters, all-around athletes. They don't necessarily need to have performance conversations all the time. It's transparent, constant conversation and communication. They're just focused on the doing. They're not getting clogged with other stuff."

But scaling the business can be particularly tricky for Crusaders because they have preferences that can confound the effort. As we have seen, they can attract followers more motivated by the mission than necessarily possessing key functional competence. Some Crusaders prefer to hire replicas of themselves or folks with whom they want to have breakfast and then do not always feel comfortable letting underperformers go.

As a Crusader, you'll find that translating your mission into a set of values that guide hiring is one of your most important tools to scale the business. Ben Cohen rued some of the hiring choices he and Jerry Greenfield made as their business was growing: "We ended up hiring people who had the skills, but not the values. What we realized was you can teach someone the skills, but you can't teach them the values. If you [look beyond] what's going to serve the company for the next little while and focus on what's really going to make us successful for the long term, you'll give values a lot more weight."

So as a Crusader, you may be wondering how to balance your tendency to remain above the fray, recruit those motivated by your mission and aligned with your values, and still ensure the operational discipline to scale the business. Katherine Hays achieved this balance, attracting talent with headroom to grow, clearly connecting task to mission, and then giving her collaborators just enough rope.

The Crusader's Gifts and Gaps

Throughout this chapter, we have seen how Crusaders build their businesses to address big problems that matter. If you're a Crusader, you have a keen appreciation for the importance of identifying and aligning common interests among customers and suppliers within your ecosystem to create a business with broad impact. You tend to find it easy to attract like-minded souls through the deep empathy, authentic relationship building, and charisma you bring to your mission. Your challenges in building for growth stem from your tendency to focus more on engaging customers, suppliers, and employees in the mission than on the operational details needed to achieve it. Meanwhile, your empathy can occasionally lead you to avoid conflict.

Let's now take a look at your core strengths and difficulties:

- **Keen awareness of misaligned relationships in complex networks:** The Crusader has a profound ability to discover the unexpressed needs and wants of others and convert them into a compelling mission of a better future. We have seen this strength manifested in the creation of hypoallergenic household products (Jessica Alba), the desire to connect the world through 140-character bursts of text (Jack Dorsey), or the Cinderella moment of young women who aspire to wear dresses they cannot afford to buy for a special event (Jenny Fleiss). As a Crusader, you often define your building task by sensing a set of emotional needs or an opportunity that can be addressed but is currently out of reach.

- **Charisma:** Your Builder Type also has enormous charisma, which helps to animate the vision. We saw this characteristic in Ben Cohen and Jerry Greenfield, who drew both employees and consumers to their own special brand of ice cream with social activism on top, and in the high-profile but flawed magnetism of Elizabeth Holmes, who attracted many to her Theranos dream. Since the mission of many Crusaders has an emotional element to it, the energy and passion of this Builder Type appeal strongly to both followers and customers. As a Crusader, you'll find your charisma to be a key element of your leadership power as you infuse the mission with your emotional connections to others.

- **Compassion and the ability to develop deep, trusting relationships:**
  Most Crusaders quickly develop deep relationships with
  employees, customers, and suppliers. This trust stems from
  Crusaders' deep listening skills and helps fuel the early traction
  of their vision. We saw this core strength in Nate Morris's approach to selling his first national account, Wegmans. Katherine
  Hays also used this skill to identify the gaps in the video-game
  environment for publishers, developers, and advertisers and to
  create enormous value for all. As a Crusader, you forge deep and
  trusting relationships, which enable you to align your customer's interests with yours and other members of your ecosystem.
  Although this gift is one of the key elements of how you create
  the initial value of your company early on, you must embed it in
  your culture to scale your business over time.

- **Tendency to assume all new revenue is good revenue:** Your passion
  for your mission and personal concern for your customers can
  lead you to take on the wrong kind of business that does not
  increase your profitability, the lifeblood of any enterprise. If
  you're a Crusader, it's easy for you to assume a mission-aligned
  customer is the source of good revenue, but if you can't generate
  an attractive profit from each customer over time, you risk the
  economic viability of the company you are building.

  All builders who are beginning to scale their businesses need
  to critically evaluate individual customer profitability. Crusaders
  are particularly susceptible to the trap of accepting lower customer profitability because of the deep empathy on which they
  build their customer relationships. In the same way you are challenged to fire underperforming employees, as a Crusader, you
  also have difficulty "firing" a customer who bet on you and your
  mission in the early going. Throughout our consulting careers

and in the case studies we teach, we see this challenge crop up with this kind of builder who feels a conflict between personal loyalty and the profitability imperative of growth and scale.

- **Difficulty in translating why to how:** As a Crusader, you are masterful in describing why your company's mission is so urgent. However, you may be less interested in, and perhaps even less innately skilled at, translating the why into the how—the operational steps necessary to realize it. When your followers seek guidance on how to do something, you are tempted—in tennis terms—to "run around your backhand" and make sure they are aligned with the mission (your preferred forehand stroke). This can lead to mistaking will for skill, or vice versa, as noted by the Center for Creative Leadership, a nonprofit global education provider headquartered in Greensboro, North Carolina. Several Crusaders we interviewed described frustration with their direct reports. After confirming the person was aligned with the organization's mission, the builders then left the person to do the job. But some direct reports needed more than mission alignment, as Greg Titus, founder of CourseAdvisor and serial investor, explains: "If you're the type of person who likes a lot of structure and a formal training program, then you need to go to a different company. It's not that you're not smart. It's just that you need a different type of an environment to be successful."

"Elevate and Delegate" Strategies to Become a Stronger Crusader

You have a choice: stand pat with the considerable skill set you have, or deepen your expertise as a builder. If you opt for the latter, here are five specific actions you can start immediately to either elevate your gifts, compensate for your gaps, or employ a mixture of both. Whatever you decide to do, you can learn from your fellow Crusaders. And in chapter 9, we'll show you how you might expand your repertoire to include aspects of the Driver, Explorer, and Captain.

1. **Press the flesh with your current and prospective talent:** The combination of your compelling vision and charisma is what draws people in. But as your business becomes more complex, many issues will pull you away from your employees and the talent you must continue to attract to realize your Crusader's mission. You should resist this gravitational force. You need to stay engaged with your team in person and often. It is your animating vision and force of character they need to keep in the forefront of all they do as they operationalize and scale your mission. In short, they need to feel connected to the banner of your mutual crusade.

   Greg Titus lives this principle by having all-hands meetings each week with the entire company. He uses these forums to celebrate both individual and team victories, and discuss openly the challenges the company is facing. He introduces new team members and places them in the center of his transparent culture—by asking them to introduce themselves and tell an embarrassing story from their past (as he himself has often done). The guard drops early in Greg's company and, as a result, he helps his employees forge deeper, more trusting bonds from the start.

2. **Be the chief listening officer:** One of your most developed talents is how you listen to your customers to discern their unexpressed needs, wants, and aspirations. This attentiveness is likely to have initiated your crusade. You need to keep doing this and mentor others in the art.

While all builders must listen to customers, the empathic bond you create with your customers as a Crusader can be a source of competitive advantage, enabling you to translate those insights into the cultural and operational elements of your business. For example, in both her video-game advertising company and her viral-video marketing company, Katherine Hays mentors her protégés in this art of creative listening.

3. **Use your brand and culture to transmit your mission and transcend your limitations:** As we have said, your charisma and character are the two animating features of your vision and mission. As your organization scales, these features are critical managerial levers to extend your mission beyond your physical reach. However, your charisma can lead some customers and employees to begin seeing you as the messiah of your mission—a viewpoint that makes your company vulnerable to your own foibles and inevitable mistakes.

   Umair Khan is a serial entrepreneur and founder of Folio3 (an offshore IT consulting firm) and of SecretBuilders (an educational game developer that "gamifies" popular books). He shared with us his approach to using culture as a way to both extend a mission and buffer his own mistakes. "Of course we hire people who are drawn to the mission. Believe in my mission, believe in our mission, but don't blindly believe in the plan. I seek to separate me as the business leader from the messenger and the visionary, because if I do wrong, everybody does wrong."

4. **Hire or partner with an operator to be your alter ego:** We have seen throughout this chapter that translating your vision into the day-to-day operating steps is often a shortcoming if you are a Crusader. One effective strategy is to delegate this critical

responsibility to someone else who shares your vision but has a penchant for execution.

For example, Doris Yeh, who with her sister founded Mirapath, a supplier to data centers, describes her Crusader approach: "I sell, she executes. We are yin and yang. I am always thinking about new ideas, and she is thinking of being a sanity check." Lest you think working with a family member is easy, Yeh attests otherwise: "Being sisters is actually very hard, but we know that the intent and the goal is always to make Mirapath better. It's a lot of discussions, fights, and arguments. But I think that discussion makes us a better team."

Aaron Levie, the CEO and cofounder of publicly traded cloud-storage company, Box, describes a similar approach: "When we were about forty-five or fifty employees, we hired a chief operating officer, and I essentially delegated most of the mechanical parts of operating the business to him so I could focus on products and strategy of where we are going as a company."

5. **Don't allow personal loyalty to inadvertently compromise growth:** As the most successful Crusaders scale their business, they begin to develop a more dispassionate relationship with their customers. Of course, this change does not affect their deeply personal relationship with their earliest customers, but the Crusaders now see the implications of maintaining these customers.

A CEO of a company that Rosemark Capital (Chris Kuenne's firm) invested in captured this tension well: "Armed with the data on how the tailored solutions we built for our earliest customers was choking the efficiency of our platform and hurting us with our larger customers, I had no choice but to have the

Crusader in Action

I believe entrepreneurship is the great equalizer.
—Marsha Firestone, Crusader, Women Presidents' Organization

Founded in 1997 by Marsha Firestone, the Women Presidents' Organization is the premier membership organization for women presidents, CEOs, and managing directors of privately held multimillion-dollar companies. The mission of the group is "to promote economic security for women, their employees and their families." Firestone had long been aware of the economic discrimination professional women experience. In 1965, when the dean of the Tulane Law School interviewed her as a prospective law student, he asked her why she wanted to apply and take the spot of a man who had to provide for his family. Later in her career, when she was on the faculty of the American Management Association, she discovered her salary was significantly below that of all of her colleagues. She recalls, "I agitated for a raise. I got eight thousand dollars, which was still probably a third of what the others were making."

It was experiences like these that fueled Firestone's Crusader zeal to pursue a PhD at Columbia, where she studied under the great Margaret Mead. Firestone's dissertation was on the role of nonverbal communication, and she aptly applied this knowledge years later in forming the Women Presidents' Organization, realizing that women leaders could learn best from one another in small groups focused on specific management challenges.

Firestone explains that when the organization first started working with women business owners, their members' objectives were simply to provide for themselves. Back then, "they didn't have a big dream. And now, women starting companies can dream the big dream."

With chapters in over 120 cities around the globe and thousands of members, Firestone is scaling a high-impact organization dedicated to a cause that can truly change the world: how best to encourage, support, and celebrate women leaders who start and lead significant business.

adult conversation and let them know we could no longer serve them." The "adult conversation" is code for an open and honest conversation expressing that the commercial relationship is no longer working. This Crusader delivered on the trust he had built with these customers. He helped them move to a smaller competitor and eased the transition to ensure uninterrupted service. So there is a way to be true to your Crusader principles but also stay focused on reducing customer complexity to enhance scalability.

These are suggestions for how you can become a more expert builder by elevating your innate strengths and buffering or delegating your weaknesses. In chapter 9, we invite you to move beyond these steps, and we challenge you to put yourself on a more ambitious path. We will suggest how you might best take on some of the specific strengths of another Builder Personality Type, make them your own, and, in so doing, become a master builder.

The Crusader's Blueprint

Profile

Factor	Description
MOTIVATION	• To solve problems that matter to society, a marketplace, or both. • Driven from a deep-seated ability to empathize with others, feeling their needs and wants and motivated to address them by creating a mission-based company.
DECISION-MAKING MODE	• Highly intuitive and driven from an emotional sense of what is right.
MANAGEMENT APPROACH	• Guided by their founding mission and intuition, Crusaders can struggle with tough people issues, as they eschew conflict and often allow underperformers to languish rather than be ushered out of the business.
LEADERSHIP STYLE	• Attracts talent to handle the more operational aspects of the business, inspiring them with vision and company mission, but not always directing them in a systematic manner.

GIFTS (Strengths)

- Inspires with bold vision conveyed with charisma.
- Willing to delegate to others.
- Comfortable with more flexible, creative workplace environment.
- Has personal touch in dealing with others.

GAPS (Weaknesses)

- Struggles with translating vision into practical to-dos.
- Vulnerable to hiring on vision enthusiasm versus competency (assuming cultural fit always).
- Conflict avoidance can let problems fester.

Strategies for Growth

Strengths and Weaknesses by Growth Dynamic

Solution: Converting Ideas into Products

+ Engages in and addresses meaningful challenges and opportunities
- Is keenly aware of misaligned interests

Team: Galvanizing Individual Talent for Collaborative Impact

+ Attracts and inspires others through charisma
+ Forges deep, trusting relationships
- Avoids conflict

Customer: Transforming Buyers into Partners

+ Forges deep, trusting relationships
- Assumes all revenue is good revenue

Sponsor: Aligning Financial and Other Supporters

+ Attracts like-minded backers
- Requires patient capital to realize the long-term vison

Scale: Elevating the Business

+ Has an audacious mission with significant scale potential
- Has difficulty translating why to how

How to Be a Stronger Builder

- "Press the flesh" with your current and prospective talent
- Be the chief listening officer
- Use your brand and culture to transmit your mission and transcend your limitations
- Hire or partner with an operator to be your alter ego
- Don't allow personal loyalty to inadvertently compromise growth

5

THE CAPTAIN

Pragmatic, Team-Enabling, and Direct

They were all surgeons, but I wanted to build a team.

—*Margery Kraus, Captain, APCO Worldwide*

Margery Kraus was a thirty-eight-year-old mother of three young children when a partner at Arnold & Porter, a well-known Washington, DC, law firm, happened to see her running a call-in program on C-SPAN. He and some of his partners asked her to take over a nascent consulting practice to serve the expanding needs of their clients.

While she immediately saw the opportunity with this role, she also could see its challenges: a team with an ill-defined mission somewhere between advocacy-like lobbying and public relations, composed of a handful of non-legal professionals, within a law firm where formal legal training was the currency of the realm. Kraus describes her first impressions: "It wasn't like I had this great design or vision. I saw an

The Captain Profile

Factor	Description
MOTIVATION	• To build an enterprise of enduring value through unleashing the productive potential of individuals and teams.
DECISION-MAKING MODE	• Dispassionate and focused on growth; careful to be consistent with mission, vision, and prior personal commitments.
MANAGEMENT APPROACH	• Direct, honest, and consistent in communication and expectations of individuals and teams.
LEADERSHIP STYLE	• Empowers others after setting clear goals and expectations, while consistently applying deeply held principles of honesty and transparency. • Consensus-driven.

opportunity, and I saw people struggling to get it done. I felt I knew what to do. I just see things and think, if you connect the dots and drive it, it will happen."[1]

Like Kraus, Captains often build ventures that either started out as someone else's brainchild or coalesced the elements of customer need, talented people, and timing into a business. As she explains, "There were clearly lobbyists, PR people, and grassroots campaign organizers, but nobody was a general practitioner. They were all surgeons. I wanted to build a team that first listened to our clients to help them diagnose their problem. It seemed just like common sense to me."

She credits much of her global success to her early experience as a teacher—a role many Captains play in building their businesses: "If you're doing business outside the US and get in trouble, it's usually because you don't understand how the system works. So being a civics teacher is actually pretty helpful."

APCO Worldwide, which Kraus spun out of the law firm many years ago, now has offices in sixty countries around the world, serving heads of state and global CEOs. It has grown to be the second-largest privately held public relations firm in the United States.

Kraus's founding story of APCO is vintage Captain. Serendipity helped to create the context, and then Kraus practiced active listening to understand the problem and recruited and galvanized the right team to forge a collaborative culture.

Culture is a very big deal for Captains, as opposed to being an afterthought for some of their builder cousins. They complement their manage-from-behind style with a lead-from-the-front approach to culture. In this way, Captains create a more cohesive team by preserving a sense of collegial, interdependent commitment to the work at hand. Kraus puts it perfectly: "I hired a lot of smart people who thought bigger than what they were doing."

How Captains Engage:
"Collaboration Beats Dictatorship"

If you're a Captain, your motivation comes from making something you deem important happen. You relish the building process itself almost as much as the businesses you build. "I've never worried about how big this firm is," Kraus says, "I've just worried about how good we are and how different we might be."

As a Captain, you're inspired to create an enterprise of value through your three core gifts: strategic vision, values, and empowering others.

You are not necessarily anchored around a particular problem (the Explorer), the market opportunity or a product inspiration (the Driver), or an ambitious sense of the market's deeper needs (the Crusader). Instead, you are drawn to the task of building through your ability to unleash the value-creating power of others.

Captains are pragmatic managers, but not usually with the me-centered or overcontrolling style of their Driver and Explorer counterparts. If you are a Captain, you are more like an orchestra conductor, comfortable in yielding the spotlight to soloists or instrumental sections as circumstances dictate, while retaining the baton of leadership and a high level of accountability for results.

Captains prefer a trust-but-verify style of decision making. This approach isn't because they don't have a strong point of view, but because they would rather find consensus through a focus on the mission and vision. In meetings, Captains may listen first and speak last, not wanting to compromise the possibility of empowering others to get the job done.

Let's look at how these elements of motivation, management, leadership, and decision-making style manifest themselves as Captains engage the five dynamics of company growth.

The Solution Dynamic:
Converting Ideas into Products

Captains present a mixed picture in the solution dynamic. Some, like Margery Kraus, fall into an idea spawned by others and start making it their own. Others, like Paul Gilbert, founder of MedAvante, a global innovator in clinical trials for mental health drugs, develop their ideas through a deliberate, often collaborative, process of focused brainstorming and trial and error.

"You need to let the steering wheel turn with the road you're discovering."

In 2001, Gilbert gathered eight accomplished friends and colleagues from marketing, technology, and the health-care industry. Each weekend for more than a year, they would brainstorm additions to a list of potential near-term health-care problems, which they believed they could build a company to solve. They finally emerged with a novel way to enhance the accuracy of clinical trials for new psychotropic drugs (think Prozac).

These drugs are very expensive to create. Clinical testing of these new compounds often fails to isolate the therapeutic effect from a placebo (sugar pill). Gilbert, the orchestrator of the venture, assembled a team of experts, created an environment of collaboration, and developed and commercialized a method to solve this seemingly intractable problem.

The story of Gilbert and his cofounder building MedAvante reveals three common tendencies of the Captain: organize a talented team; use a methodical, fact-based approach; and focus on material economic problems that represent a near-term business opportunity. This approach stands in stark contrast to the Driver, who believes he or she can sense where the market is headed and who creates products, services, and solutions often in advance of expressed demand.

Also in contrast with their other three builder counterparts, Captains are quite comfortable with engaging potential customers at a very early stage, even with crude prototypes of their ideas. As Gilbert says, "Entrepreneurship is a discovery process. You come to understand that the initial questions may be different from the right questions. You have to have a starting point—a clear, measurable point of pain and a value proposition that can address it. But the great majority of the time, it is not where you end up. You need to let the steering wheel turn with the road you're discovering; you cannot lock your steering wheel to a predetermined plan. It's not a road map."

In a sense, Captains face all five growth dynamics with a pragmatic, real-time approach, rather than with a predetermined sense of what the outcome should be, as Drivers and Explorers often do. In MedAvante's case, this search for the best way to demonstrate their idea became a multiyear odyssey to discover, develop, and prove the right solution to the problem they originally identified.

Just like Margery Kraus's somewhat accidental introduction to APCO, Captains may not start with a specific product or solution in mind, but they are drawn into the search for one that works. John Crowley, who developed a novel approach to clinical trials for a debilitating disease, also followed the idea-to-product path, but for far more personal and urgent reasons, as we will explain below.

"I had no choice. I had to do this . . . now!"

Imagine if your child had a rare and apparently incurable disease. What would you do? What risks might you take to find a treatment or cure for him or her? You'd probably search everywhere for any way to help your child, and you would be willing to spend whatever resources you had in that effort, right?

Now imagine you're not a doctor or scientist and you have no academic or professional background in that disease. You work for a pharmaceutical company, but you're a manager and marketer by training. Would you quit your high-paying, successful job and interrupt your career to start a company to find a cure for your child's disease?

That's what Crowley did after two of his children were diagnosed with Pompe disease, a fatal neuromuscular disorder in which children live short and excruciatingly painful lives. Crowley and his wife simply couldn't wait for others to find a cure or treatment. They needed to do something fast. Before his children were born, he had thought that sometime later in his career, he might start a company. "I'm naturally a risk-averse kind of guy," he says. "But my kids' condition left me no choice. I had to do this . . . now!"

Crowley learned of a fledgling biotech research company in Oklahoma City called Novazyme Pharmaceuticals, which was investigating a bioengineered replacement for the enzyme that is deficient in people with Pompe disease. He quit his job at Bristol-Myers Squibb and joined the Novazyme team in order to raise the capital, expedite clinical trials to demonstrate the efficacy of this enzyme approach, and get approval for its use. It was, in fact, an effective way to treat Pompe disease, though not a cure. But it was enough to save Crowley's kids' lives.

As a Captain, you may enter the solution dynamic with less clarity than other builders might have about the problem, the solution, or the business concept. However, the combination of your pragmatic business sense and your ability to galvanize a team around a question or an opportunity quickly unleashes the solution-generating power of others. With this energy, you can build a company and drive impact.

At the same time, your predilection to allow context and consensus to frame the solution may come at the expense of genuine commercial breakthroughs. Your approach can result in more incremental solutions to more immediate problems. It is less likely to lead to a Steve Jobs–like or Henry Ford–caliber truly disruptive innovation. Other Builder Personality Types probably have a better shot at those kinds of leaps.

The Team Dynamic:
Galvanizing Individual Talent for Collaborative Impact

If you're a Captain, you are as much a team assembler as you are a catalyst. You are intent on creating a company culture around values and mutual accountability. Comfortable with leading from behind, you trust your colleagues and culture to fulfill the vision for the company whose future you share. Unlike Explorers and Drivers, you find gratification in the *we* rather than the *me*. But as a Captain, you lead your teams with a trust-but-verify style that complements your focus on shared vision and values.

As difficult as it is for any builder to assemble a founding team of talented and dedicated colleagues, the challenges of attracting, retaining—and yes, pruning—the right talent to fuel growth are constant. Teams need to be recruited as well as rebooted from time to time.

And although Captains prefer a collaborative, consensus style of leadership and management, they know where they want the ship to go and what they must do to get there. They are motivated to build enterprises of enduring value by unleashing the productive potential of individuals and teams, even though circumstances sometimes force them to take the helm themselves to weather a storm or crisis.

John Crowley's current company, Amicus, offers one such example. In the summer of 2013, his young daughter was having back surgery. Crowley was sleeping on the floor in the hospital room to be with her. His business was in crisis, financially and scientifically, and Crowley had to chart a course.

He recalls, "And then one day, early in the morning, I grabbed a pen and piece of paper and said, 'Okay, lots of options. This is what we're going to do: Disentangle ourselves from our big pharma partner and largest shareholder, fire our chief science officer, close our San Diego facility, let go of another twenty-five percent of the company, and raise money from a hedge fund at a brutally dilutive rate.' The board signed up for all of it, and I executed all five of those pieces within forty-eight hours."

That moment in the hospital room is classic Captain. Even under extraordinary pressure, this Captain's pragmatic focus remained. He thought clearly to develop his plan. And because of the trust and alignment Crowley had worked hard to forge with his board, he could move swiftly and boldly.

In the ensuing months, Crowley basically refounded the company with a skeletal crew. "I think all those people who ultimately stayed, believed," he says. "It wasn't just the financial reward. We were proactively putting a pretty bold plan in place. We weren't just taking our punches and letting things happen."

If you are a corporate Captain, your leadership, management, and decision-making strengths make you a solid candidate to assume the Captain's chair in an internal venture—even if the animating idea wasn't yours to begin with. Perhaps it's an internal project around an early prototype developed in your lab, or a fledgling new business scouting team backed by the executive suite. However it manifests itself, in our experience, it is important to let executive management know you'd like this kind of opportunity, so when one comes along, you may be considered to take the helm.

We saw this exact scenario unfold in a large energy company we advised. Our team had identified a promising new business idea that required a far more entrepreneurial style of leadership than the company was used to, with a different set of metrics and talents commensurate with the competitive obstacles this team would face. Rather than choose an outsider, the CEO tapped an up-and-coming executive with no prior startup experience, but with the widespread respect she could draw on in assembling her new team. Her insider credibility enabled her to quickly organize an effective cadre around her. These efforts in turn accelerated both the business idea's time to market and the company's ability to turn this idea into a multi-million-dollar venture in short order.

As a corporate Captain, you also know that success depends on the caliber of the team you recruit for the new venture. Watch for signs that your superiors or peers may sandbag your efforts by sloughing off B- or C-level talent to your fledgling undertaking. The venture you lead is likely to attract a lot of attention, even envy, among your peers. But remember, you're not playing for the intramural championship here; you'll be competing against outside pro players at every position. Make sure your team has the right mix of inside and outside draft picks you can coach to win.

Whether you are a Captain operating within your own stand-alone new business or are a corporate captain, you know the power of principle and the cohesion provided by culture—especially when you need to draw on these in times of crisis. You use both of these tools to attract, inspire and galvanize talent to create collectively and build for growth.

For those of you who are bored sitting through yet another PowerPoint presentation, especially after you've seen a few visually engaging TED-style talks, meet Peter Arvai. He's more of a hybrid builder, blending both Captain and Crusader characteristics as a cofounder of Prezi, the software resource that helps over 75 million users—including many TED speakers—present their ideas more effectively. Born in Sweden to Hungarian parents, Peter noted that, growing up, "The word 'entrepreneur' did not exist in my vocabulary."

Through various projects and ventures, he has long been inspired by this mission of "combining storytelling and technology to help people make better decisions." He combines that Crusader's fascination with a Captain's focus on creating an authentic and unique culture of collaboration across multiple offices with employees from twenty-eight national backgrounds. "Purpose is the leading thing for me," he says, and uses that to align his "middle way" leadership and management style—patience and support for his people while challenging and pushing them to new heights.

Captain in Action

To win in the twenty-first century, you must empower others.
—Jack Ma, Alibaba

Jack Ma, the leading founder of Alibaba, captured the Captain's collaborative style by assembling seventeen of his friends in his apartment and convincing them to invest in the idea that would become the largest e-commerce site on the planet.[2] After fifteen years of tireless work and on the eve of the group's initial public offering, Ma said to his employees, "After we go public, we will continue to adhere to the principle of 'customer first, employee second, shareholder third.'"

He knows what it's like to be on the other side of success. "I flunked my exam for university two times before I was accepted by what was considered my city's worst university," Ma reminisces. On graduating with a degree in English, he was rejected from twelve jobs for which he had applied, including one at KFC, before being hired as a schoolteacher earning just $12 a month.

Considered a failure by many, Ma was blessed with a far more important talent than getting good grades. "In my university," he says, "I was elected student chairman and later became chairman of the city's Students Federation." So after two failed ventures and nothing to his name, Ma was nonetheless able to convince friends to back him.

Captains excel at empowering the people around them. As mentioned, they believe in *we* before *me* and use their extroverted nature to win friends as much as followers. They welcome collaboration and experimentation and seek input constantly.

These builders are deliberate in using their command authority and persona as well as their collegial style to inspire others for the benefit of their companies. "To win in the twenty-first century, you must empower others," Ma says. "Then they love and respect you because you made their life important."

The Customer Dynamic:
Transforming Buyers into Partners

If you're a Captain, you may not be as directly or obsessively focused on convincing customers of your idea, solution, or mission as your Driver, Explorer, or Crusader counterparts are. They each see the customer as their point of validation. Of course, like all business builders, Captains think about customers, but more to understand the business model and how they themselves can create and extract value from the market. Let's see how one Captain's approach played out in the blueprinting business.

"We won't bid on your request for a proposal, thank you very much."

For fifteen years, Suri Suriyakumar, CEO of ARC Document Solutions, had been acquiring and rolling up a series of mom-and-pop architectural blueprint-making companies in the commercial construction industry. Where the value in this industry was once centered on service and the delivery of architectural designs on ammonia-stained paper, it has shifted in the digital age. Suriyakumar is a classic Captain. He has used his pragmatic business skills to identify a new set of problems physical blueprints cannot solve, but which his teams and their relationships can.

Captains are quite good at staying true to their company vision in guiding which business to pursue. Suriyakumar's company was invited to submit a proposal for an $8 billion construction firm in Australia. On reading the specifications of the RFP, he and his team elected not to submit a proposal. They felt the client was seeking the wrong solution. This decision astonished the prospective customer, which moved forward with another vendor. Several months later, the CEO of that company called Suriyakumar and asked him why he had not submitted a proposal. Suriyakumar explained he felt the company was thinking about the problem entirely wrong: seeking price concessions for higher volumes of conventional blueprints.

The astonished CEO, who had never before been rebuffed by a vendor, invited Suriyakumar to fly to Australia to share his point of view. After listening intently to the CEO's description of the business model, Suriyakumar then applied his own practical business logic. He explained that creating additional analog blueprints that would be used once and then relegated to a storage facility for decades was not a long-term solution for this global construction company. Rather, they should move all of their construction plans to a digital format and store them in the cloud so the information could be accessed throughout the useful life of the building and later to inform future construction companies, which would be called to either renovate or demolish the building. Suriyakumar and his team ended up winning the contract and forging a far deeper partnership than they ever could have created had they just competed for the original RFP.

As a Captain, you know the power of "listen first." This instinct serves you well in both customer-facing and employee-engaging settings. It allows solutions and strategies to emerge from conversation, while demonstrating you have heard your customer or employee. You make them feel respected. You know that this engaged listening in turn breeds commitment, turning mere buyers into partners. It is your pattern of engagement that sometimes trumps the Driver's product excellence, the Explorer's solution wizardry, or even the Crusader's noble cause.

The Sponsor Dynamic:
Aligning Financial and Other Supporters

In many ways, as a Captain, you are the favored son or daughter of financial sponsors, particularly for those who back well-led teams rather than ideas or markets. Your Builder Personality Type often has the seasoned wisdom that allows you to recruit and inspire teams that build companies of significant value, the dream of most investors. You are careful to maintain your credibility with investors, believing that everyone should be from Missouri (the Show Me State).

George McLaughlin is a highly successful serial entrepreneur, angel investor, and now builder and chairman of the board of American Specialty Foods. Like many Captains, he focuses on what is, rather than speculating on what might be. On the topic of financial projections, McLaughlin says, "When I started my career, I said, 'I'm never gonna look at a projected profit and loss statement.' They always have the appearance of precision, which leads people to over-believe in them, and yet the real business just never plays out that way."

The following section describes how a Captain's pragmatism and instinct for alignment, and the deep trust he engenders, can convert even a supplier into a source of capital.

Captain in Action

Teams need captains, and vice versa—if you want to get things done.
—*Mark Coopersmith, Sony e-commerce*

When someone mentions the brand Sony, most of us think of great televisions and the PlayStation video-gaming console. Few of us think of e-commerce platforms. This is the story of a global consumer electronics brand actually inventing and ultimately spinning off just such a platform, which was created under the leadership of a corporate Captain named Mark Coopersmith.

It was the mid-1990s. Amazon was just getting under way as a books-only e-tailer. Most major players were not really sure how much effort to put into this new arena, given potential channel conflict. But Sony knew it needed to sell its products online. It also needed someone with a get-things-done reputation to spearhead this initiative.

The company assigned Coopersmith, an executive vice president of one of Sony's business units, to the job. He was already working with most of the company's electronics and content businesses. While all these businesses had started promoting products online, no group was yet selling directly to customers.

Coopersmith assembled a hybrid team of inside and outside engineers, product experts, marketers, and merchandisers. Comfortable with delegating, he became the orchestrator rather than the driver of the effort. He was, in effect, captain of a Lewis-and-Clark-style scouting team into the then frontier of the World Wide Web—dispatching his colleagues to identify and evaluate incumbent e-commerce solutions in the market.

He asked them if Sony should buy or build this new platform. Their answer: build. He then captained his team of programmers and online marketers while also running interference for them with senior management across Sony. Similar to today's lean-startup approach, Coopersmith's team had an early Sony web store up and running, securely accepting credit cards online within a very short time.

The team was located in San Francisco, away from Sony's more formal US headquarters culture in New York. As Chris Pinkham understood when he was cracking the code for Amazon Web Services, physical (and cultural) distance from the mother ship can be a key element of the corporate builder's success.

Leaders in other industries—companies like Hewlett-Packard, Pizza Hut, and BMW—were trying to figure out how to sell and serve customers online and soon asked about licensing Sony's technology. These inquiries forced a strategic choice for Sony: keep the technology for its own use, or spin it out. Sony opted for the latter strategy.

Coopersmith went from corporate Captain to startup Captain. He raised outside funding from a group of investors and later sold the company for a handsome return. After a series of subsequent transactions, the platform his team built is now part of Google.

"Turn your supplier into an investor so you can roll up your competitors."

The blueprinting industry was composed of thousands of small geographically distributed businesses, most of which were being run by their original owners, who were getting close to retirement age. With their fundamental business model and underlying technology in decline, most of these small-business owners faced limited prospects for cashing out, despite their solid regional customer network.

Suriyakumar saw an opportunity to create value by rolling up these businesses and thereby creating scale, operating efficiencies, and geographic scope advantages to serve national construction companies. He also saw the chance to upgrade both the management and the overall professionalism of these operations. He figured the increased efficiency could quickly translate into bottom-line profit and the geographic reach would accelerate revenue. Aside from the challenge of convincing these owners to sell their businesses, he also needed the capital to do it.

Suriyakumar realized he might be able to solve two problems at once—lower his supply costs and get the capital to launch this roll-up strategy. Not surprisingly for a business that was still paper-based, paper is the largest single expense. Suriyakumar went to his paper distributor on the West Coast with the following proposition: "I can give you all the paper volume from three different blueprinting companies. By consolidating all this volume with you and taking it away from your competitor, you will become one of the largest distributors in your market. I just need you to help me finance the three acquisitions."

He further leveraged his buying power with this supplier-turned-investor by negotiating a 10 percent price discount in return for a three-year paper contract. This is Captain-style value creation. Identify the opportunity to create value, leverage relationship and negotiating skills, and—voilà!—an enormous amount of value creation out of thin air.

As a Captain, you seek alignment and win-win arrangements, unlike Drivers, who tend to see the game in more zero-sum terms, in which each win tends to come at someone else's expense. Your approach is also different from that of Explorers, who are more intrigued by the system and its mechanics and are less likely to think win-win. Finally, your Crusader cousins also seek alignment in the ecosystem, but often tend to do so more through mission than economic interests.

The Scale Dynamic:
Elevating the Business

If you are a Captain, you are well equipped to anticipate and handle the challenges of this growth dynamic. You're a pragmatist, unlikely to remain enamored with your product, solution, or mission if circumstances warrant otherwise. This is not to say you improvise everything; your decision making is deliberate and disciplined.

You are willing to upgrade systems, procedures, and technology and switch out underperformers, all in the quest of growth. You build a strong culture as one of the key mechanisms to convert mission into something tangible and emotionally motivating that everyone can get behind. You imprint your personality on your organization by attracting others, directing them through a clear mission and vision and maintaining a transparent, direct relationship based on clarity of responsibility and corresponding accountability. In other words, culture is not just a nice-to-have for you; it is a platform for scaling the enterprise.

"I recruit employees according to their values, by getting to know how they live their lives."

Cindy Monroe, builder and CEO of Thirty-One Gifts, is an archetypal Captain in this regard. The genesis of her business was a discussion with one of her friends from church in Chattanooga, Tennessee. They thought if they could help their friends generate $200 to $300 more each month, they would ease the financial challenges of raising a family. Monroe created a handbag, and her friend hosted a party with other women from church to see how many might be interested in purchasing it. The company name came from the biblical inspiration for this simple help-each-other idea, Proverbs 31. That business is now on its way to generating $1 billion in sales, with more than a hundred thousand women hosting similar parties each year.

Monroe's management skills were often tested as she scaled this juggernaut of a business. One of the more profound challenges happened four years after she founded the company, when she realized she needed a more retail-savvy employee base. She moved the company from Chattanooga to Columbus, Ohio. Her dedication to her early employees was so deep that her company relocated more than twenty families to Ohio.

With clarity of mission and expectations for integrated team-based performance, she soon discovered that some of these dedicated employees lacked the skills necessary to continue scaling the business. She explains, "We hired friends who helped us grow the business in the early days, but as the business grew we needed different skill sets and had to encourage some of our closest friends to move on to other opportunities." Team first, but not at the expense of performance.

Cindy explains, "I recruit employees according to their values, by getting to know how they live their lives and how they make business decisions." Her business is increasingly dependent on a headquarters staff tightly in synch with the company mission. The approach seems to be working for her and the company's legions of party hosts.

Captain in Action

You can't ask others to invest more than you're investing yourself.
—*Chris Bischof, Eastside College Preparatory School*

Builders start and grow nonprofit ventures as well as for-profit businesses. For them, organizational survival may be just as important a success indicator as scale is for businesses. By that measure, Chris Bischof, the Captain who built Eastside College Preparatory School, now entering its third decade in economically challenged East Palo Alto, California, demonstrates the importance of this style of team engagement. He humbly credits his team's shared passion about the school's expanding mission, but his own team-first, lead-by-example style speaks volumes about the importance of his ongoing frontline engagement: "I think the most effective leaders are those who lead by example. You can't ask others to invest more than you're investing yourself. For me, one of the most rewarding aspects of leading an organization is the shared commitment among our staff. Together we're learning through experience and coming up with creative solutions to address the challenges we face in meeting our goals. I think getting the participation of everyone involved leads to a much more fulfilling working environment and far better solutions than any one of us could develop on our own."

That's a Captain talking, for sure.

"The *we* is stronger than the *me*."

Margery Kraus, the Captain who built APCO Worldwide, describes her approach to scaling through culture: "If you believe in culture, then you have to go out and preserve it. You have to hire the right people. You have to make sure they understand what the values of the company are, and you have to carry that forward. You can walk into an APCO office almost anywhere in the world, and the culture will surround you. People left good jobs to come into the firm because they saw something very different. To do that, everybody had to believe in a common set of values: the *we* is stronger than the *me*."

That's a Captain speaking. If you're a Captain, the cultural values you instill in your team help you achieve scale. A collaborative culture allows you to hire, empower others, and expand the company at a rate not often possible using any other method. It is one of the keys to your success.

The Captain's Gifts and Gaps

As a Captain, you often start building a new business by identifying and exploiting commonsense-based commercial opportunities (even if the idea wasn't yours originally), but you are careful not to crowd out your team. In this regard, you are unlike Drivers and Explorers, who attach their egos to commercial success and systematic solutions, respectively. You tend to stay above the fray, a vantage point that can strengthen your focus on people and teams. However, in fast-changing and highly competitive markets, this tendency can potentially leave your venture vulnerable.

Here is a quick summary of your gifts and gaps:

- **Forming and empowering the team:** As a Captain, you are attuned to what motivates your team. You apply your considerable listening skills and understanding of the way others take on responsibility and feel accountable, and you deftly deploy the right people to the right assignments to get the most out of their talents. We saw this gift on full display in how Margery Kraus connected her APCO team to serve her firm's clients through collaborating in a way other firms had not discovered. This integration of different skills, cultivated by Kraus, allowed her to lead APCO's emergence as a market leader.

- **Managing through vision alignment:** One of your most effective tools in achieving alignment with both internal teams and external suppliers and customers is your clarity and consistency in managing according to the vision. We saw how important vision alignment was to Paul Gilbert in his building and scaling of MedAvante and to Suriyakumar as he leveraged supplier financing to roll up blueprinting firms.

- **Willingness to make the tough calls on people:** The complementary strength to empowering your team is that you don't hesitate to remove underperformers. We saw John Crowley do this at a key juncture in building Amicus, when he realized he did not have all the right people on his team. Cindy Monroe did the same at Thirty-One Gifts, even after she had moved close friends—some of whom, she later discovered, were not cut out for the next chapter of growth for her company—all the way to Columbus from Chattanooga.

- **Overreliance on consensus:** One risk for Captains involves how much empowerment you afford your team. This challenge can be particularly damaging in fast-moving markets, when rapid, decisive action is required. While Crowley is a shining counter-example of this pitfall, many Captains tend to wait too long to act as they garner the consensus that makes them comfortable to act. Corporate Captains are particularly vulnerable to this challenge.

- **Remaining too far from the action:** There can be a fine line between delegation and falling out of touch with your customers, your competitors, and the market in general. Your behind-the-scenes style can leave you too far removed from the front lines, where your company and its competitors are addressing real customer needs and are developing solutions for those needs.

- **Accepting incrementalism as a substitute for innovation:** While you have a good nose for the next commercial opportunity to serve or expand your relationship with current customers, it's important you don't allow your team just to satisfice, that is, to meet only the minimum response to a need, particularly in rapidly changing markets. Mercurial markets can require a bolder and more aggressive pursuit of new ideas.

So what can you do now to start improving your overall effectiveness as a Captain? Here are six actions you can take, depending on your preference for elevating your gifts, compensating for your gaps, or employing some mix of both.

"Elevate and Delegate" Strategies to Become a Stronger Captain

1. **Keep a sharp eye out for the next champion on your already-solid team:** Your building strength relies on enormously talented team members inspired by you and your vision for the company. Chris Dries is a Captain and the CEO of United

Silicon Carbide, a developer and manufacturer of silicon chips that enable higher power efficiency for a greener product. The story of how he hired his vice president of engineering, who he says was "the best guy I've ever worked with in my career," typifies this gift of recognizing potential talent. "Hiring him was a pivotal moment," he says. "It's hard to explain how transformative that one individual was in the early stages of this business."

First, Dries invited this executive, who headed up the engineering function of a publicly traded company, to interview Dries's nascent team—a step that immediately demonstrated the open and honest culture he had forged. After an intensive weekend with Dries and his team, this enormously talented engineering leader was convinced of the team's value. He not only joined the team, but also invested in the company, contributing a significant check to the next round of financing. Dries's aiming high in the talent game and his enfranchising such a player represent an invaluable Captain technique.

2. **Share the Captain's chair to show and teach others how you lead:** With your direct, honest, consistent communication, you are arguably the most effective leader of all Builder Types. You set clear goals and expectations and then delegate responsibility for execution. This form of leadership comes to you intuitively, but others not so naturally endowed can learn much from you. Pick out a few individuals (perhaps at different levels of the organization), and take them under your wing—almost like students you are coaching.

   You'll need to do more than just model this approach; you'll need to explain it and compare notes with your mentees on its finer points. You might allow them to shadow you for a week or maybe give them a spot at the table where they can practice your Captain's repertoire under your watchful eye—a kind of "Captain for the meeting" session. Although your leadership talents are distinctive, some of them are teachable in more structured training contexts focused on collaborative leadership skills.

We understand you're running a business, not a business school. But your leadership style is a resource that can be leveraged into a value-creating, even value-transforming, resource—precisely because it can unleash your colleagues' latent creative talent and ingenuity other Builder Types may struggle to capture.

3. **Avoid confusing your teams with your twin strengths of listening and consensus building:** Your *we*-over-*me* default style can open up the reservoir of creativity and commitment that sparks future innovation and creates an environment in which slipups and failures may be more openly acknowledged. However, some of your followers can mistake your patient listening and preference for consensus as an indication you are not prepared to make tough, unpleasant decisions when necessary.

   Having seen only your velvet glove, they may be surprised—and even disillusioned—if circumstances call for an iron fist from time to time. Make sure your colleagues understand your actions when you use this technique, because, otherwise, it can confuse or even scare them into the very kind of silent obedience you probably don't want.

4. **Remember that consensus is wonderful, except when it's not:** While your leadership is often strengthened by your ability to forge consensus, sometimes you must go it alone. Yet those are precisely the times when you can leverage the trust you have built

to win over your naysayers after the fact. As described earlier, John Crowley needed to do exactly this to reorient—indeed even jumpstart again—his company, using the game plan he had fashioned from those lonely moments in his child's hospital room.

Your consensus management style can be powerful. But when quick decisions on complex issues are called for, such an approach can be problematic. Think of the price firms like BlackBerry and Nokia paid for their version of indecision—in both cases caught like deer in Apple's headlights.[3] Even in slower-moving markets, like the inexorable digital takeover of film photography, a culture of consensus—reinforced by complacency and self-confidence—can prove fatal, as it did for both Kodak and Polaroid. Crises and consensus often don't go together.

June Ressler, builder of Cenergy International Services, a Houston-based staffing and consulting agency serving the energy and offshore drilling sector, is a good role model for her fellow Captains in this regard. Ressler told us she doesn't like relying on written sales reports: "It's so funny, my brain doesn't work like that. The only way I get comfort is I listen to our sales call every Monday morning from eight thirty to nine thirty, while I am driving to work—so I'm in my car and I'm listening. When I get in the car, I say [to myself], 'I am not going to say a word this time,' and then invariably I'm, like, pushing mute, 'Oh and by the way, did you do that?' You know, I just can't help myself." So sometimes even a consensus-oriented Captain can't resist taking a more Driver-esque stance. In this case, perhaps that's not surprising—Ressler is a former practicing lawyer who races Formula 4 cars in her spare time.

5. **Push your teams to look beyond incremental improvements:** Your pragmatic focus on what's next suits you well at making steady progress on many fronts. But gradualism can foster a kind of inadvertent complacency and a false sense of confidence if your fundamental business, business model, or technology is stagnating or in decline.

Not all members of your team may have the skill, insight, or guts to interpret and synthesize the kind of emerging signals the marketplace can send. Time constraints can inhibit the team's ability to get up to speed, consider options, and, ultimately, make a decision. But you bear the leader's responsibility to see for yourself and to keep track of those "disturbances in the Force"—as Obi-Wan Kenobi of *Star Wars* might say—that may prove your undoing. And that means getting out of the building, meeting with customers, and checking out competitors and startups geographically or competitively near you—regardless of the scouting reports you may have been getting from inside your inner circle.

In Paul Gilbert's case at MedAvante, he realized he must avoid the complacency trap and coalesced his team around a gut-wrenching and bet-the-company Captain's call. His company had been focused entirely on measuring the efficacy of new prospective mental health drugs, a therapeutic area that was showing troubling signs of slowing, though still profitable. Gilbert decided to divert scarce resources to develop a clinical testing protocol to measure the effectiveness of new Alzheimer's drugs. The payoff? In Gilbert's words, "We won something like eleven of the next thirteen contracts, so as psychiatry was shrinking rapidly, we were able to pivot into Alzheimer's, which was a large and growing area . . . [H]ad we not . . . gone after Merck [the original Alzheimer's disease contractor], we wouldn't be here today—because psychiatry shrank too far, too fast."

6. **Renew your trust-but-verify style by personal example:** As a Captain, you probably have an almost instinctive feel for the importance of establishing trust in your organizational culture. You get what the Great Place To Work Institute (the company behind those "Great Places To Work" lists in *Fortune* and other publications around the world) has found: trust is essential, both vertically between bosses and workers and horizontally among peers.[4] But that trust, while hard to build, is easy to lose if you're not constantly renewing it through working side by side with your team.

As a Captain, consider the suggestions we offer as a starting point for how you can become a stronger builder. Each suggestion is a function of our having analyzed, worked with, and invested in many Captains. However, your growth opportunities are unique to you. The generalizable point is that you have many leadership gifts. These tend to enhance the alignment and performance of your team on day-to-day issues, but as we've seen with each Builder Personality, various dispositions also have their drawbacks. If you are a Captain, your personality can lead to incremental, rather than bold growth. We encourage you to consider our further suggestions in chapter 9 in your pursuit of becoming a master builder.

The Captain's Blueprint

Profile

Factor	Description
MOTIVATION	• To build an enterprise of enduring value through unleashing the productive potential of individuals and teams.
DECISION-MAKING MODE	• Dispassionate and focused on growth; careful to be consistent with mission, vision, and prior personal commitments.
MANAGEMENT APPROACH	• Direct, honest, and consistent in communication and expectations of individuals and teams.
LEADERSHIP STYLE	• Empowers others after setting clear goals and expectations, while consistently applying deeply held principles of honesty and transparency. • Consensus-driven.

GIFTS (Strengths)

- Empowers others within regimen of clear accountability.
- Encourages team member candor.
- Willing to share credit for positive outcomes.
- Open to "bubble-up" creativity versus top-down direction.

GAPS (Weaknesses)

- Comfort with delegating can remove Captain from important frontline developments.
- May allow search for consensus to postpone fast decisions.
- Focus on steady improvement may miss big-scale outside trends.

Strategies for Growth

Strengths and Weaknesses by Growth Dynamic

Solution: Converting Ideas into Products

+ Pragmatic approach
− Tends to adopt incrementalism as a substitute for innovation

Team: Galvanizing Individual Talent for Collaborative Impact

+ Forms empowered teams with less dependency on star talent
+ Is comfortable making tough people decisions
− Can be overly reliant on consensus

Customer: Transforming Buyers into Partners

+ Delivers value consistently
+ Is transparent and direct
− Tendency to satisfice rather than innovate

Sponsor: Aligning Financial and Other Supporters

+ Has a track record of delivering results
+ Recruits, manages, and directs strong teams
− Can get crosswise with aggressive investors

Scale: Elevating the Business

+ Focuses on execution
− May miss market shifts in fast-moving industries

How to Be a Stronger Builder

- Keep a sharp eye out for the next champion on your already-solid team
- Share the Captain's chair to show and teach others how you lead
- Avoid confusing your teams with your twin strengths of listening and consensus building
- Remember that consensus is wonderful, except when it's not
- Push your teams to look beyond incremental improvements
- Renew your trust-but-verify style by personal example

PART TWO

ASSEMBLING YOUR BEST CREWS FOR GROWTH

Finding Those Who Best Leverage Your Builder Personality

Our book decodes what we believe is the central factor in building long-lasting businesses of significant scale—the personality of the builder. But every successful builder needs a crew—in fact, many crews, each with its own role, resources, and requirements. In building a physical structure, one crew might dig the foundation while others focus on framing, wiring, or plumbing. Still others assemble the financing package. Building a large-scale business structure is not fundamentally different. No business builder creates a successful, durable, and valuable enterprise alone. After all, there is no such word as "solopreneur."

"Entre" is the mantra here: *entre*preneurship requires collaborative connections *between* people and resources. In part 2 of this book, we offer practical advice to each Builder Personality on how you can best select and work more effectively with the three groups of people who have the greatest multiplier effect for your business—your cobuilder if you choose to have one (or more), your key employees, and your primary investors or executive backers.

This is all about builder–crew fit—improving your odds of best complementing and reinforcing your Builder Personality for the ultimate benefit of the company's success to which both you and your crew aspire. Builders who confuse loyalty with competency, or crew members who default to sycophancy rather than genuine collaboration, both destroy value.

The next three chapters offer a pragmatic guide to how these collaborations can work well. We start in chapter 6 with your most personal choice, whether and how to pick a cobuilder to share the building challenge with you. In chapter 7, we pull back our lens a bit more, to include the other key members of your building crew. Finally, in chapter 8, we suggest how you can match your agenda and building style with that of the primary outside financial or inside executive sponsors you need, whether in a startup or corporate venture. Part 2 is comprised of the following 3 chapters:

Chapter 6   **Partnering with Cobuilders:**
                   Choosing Collaborators Who Fit You Best

Chapter 7   **Recruiting Your Inside Team:**
                   Selecting the People Who Work Best with You

Chapter 8   **Attracting Your Best Financial Sponsors:**
                   Powering Vision with the Right Capital

6

PARTNERING WITH COBUILDERS

Choosing Collaborators Who Fit You Best

"Best blind date ever!"

That's how SoulCycle cobuilder Julie Rice described her initial meeting over lunch with Elizabeth Cutler.[1] The women were looking for an innovative alternative to indoor fitness clubs—where members could mix social networking and fun while pedaling off calories. Rice explained the genesis of their concept and partnership: "[Elizabeth and I] talked about creating an entirely new exercise concept, a fitness 'experience' designed to be physically challenging, emotionally uplifting, and spiritually inspiring. And more than anything, we wanted to make it fun. We talked about chic design, cool branding, and a departure from all things people found frustrating about gyms. We sketched a rough business plan on a napkin and agreed to meet again the following week. When I walked outside, my head was spinning. I hailed a taxi, and before I could even close the door, my phone rang. It was Elizabeth. 'I'm going to look for a rental space; you research towels.' Five months later, we were open."

Their husbands also got involved, one as chief marketing officer and the other as the creator of the brand name. Fast (or more appropriately, spin) forward nine years. The two cobuilders sold SoulCycle to Equinox in 2011 for a handsome sum, and by 2016, the company had almost ninety locations and more than four hundred thousand pedaling customers.

Rice, like a Captain, attributes Cutler's and her success to their differences and their synergy: "We're complete opposites. We just happen to have incredible business chemistry. I'm conservative and risk averse. Elizabeth is a baller [read Driver]. When you're honest about your strengths and weaknesses and accept your role in the organization, there's no toe stepping, no ego issues, and things run much more efficiently."

Starting a business, much less building it into a large and durable enterprise, is never easy, and it's often a lonely endeavor. It's no surprise many builders—perhaps you included—choose to embark on that adventure with cofounders. That's a decision that immediately puts the issue of Builder Personality front and center—for both of you.

Just take a look at this partial list of cobuilders:

Apple: Steve Jobs and Steve Wozniak

Microsoft: Bill Gates and Paul Allen

Ben & Jerry's: Ben Cohen and Jerry Greenfield

Intel: Gordon Moore and Bob Noyce

P & G: William Procter and James Gamble

Airbnb: Nathan Blecharczyk, Brian Chesky, and Joe Gebbia

Google: Sergey Brin and Larry Page

Rent the Runway: Jenn Hyman and Jenny Fleiss

Warby Parker: Neil Blumenthal, Dave Gilboa, Andrew Hunt, and Jeffrey Raider

Pinterest: Ben Silbermann, Evan Sharp, and Paul Sciarra

Eventbrite: Julia Hartz and Kevin Hartz

HP: Bill Hewlett and Dave Packard

These builder partnerships cut across industry, geographic, gender, and cultural lines. This chapter discusses the potential and perils of the delicate but intense cobuilder relationship. The matchups highlight the importance of understanding—and respecting—how Builder Personality shapes the entrepreneurial process. More specifically, we'll show you how to deal with three big issues: choosing the right cobuilder, collaborating with him or her (or them), and flagging potential conflicts between and among you.

Marriage by Another Name

Presumably you would not rush into marriage without really knowing your prospective spouse. You'd want to be compatible on the issues that matter, trust each other, have similar goals for the marriage, and be able to handle and resolve disagreements, among other matters. And here's a builder reality check: especially in the early years of building a business, you are likely to spend more waking hours with your cobuilder than with your spouse. And unfortunately for the ideal of marital bliss, those business marriages may outlast the domestic ones. Divorce of either kind is not a desired outcome. So getting to know your prospective cobuilder—his or her gifts, gaps, games, quirks, and character—is important stuff for both your sanity and the success of your business.

Have you and your potential partner worked with one another before in high-stress situations? Have you—like Bill Gates and Paul Allen, Ben Cohen and Jerry Greenfield, or Howard Lerman and his rowboat mates—been friends since high school? Maybe you met in college or graduate school, like Sergey Brin and Larry Page or Jenn Hyman and Jenny Fleiss, or went camping together on a two-week wilderness trip, like Bill Hewlett and Dave Packard. Perhaps you've worked closely together, as did the cobuilders of Pixar and Intel. Or just happened to meet over lunch and—like SoulCycle's cofounders—had a gut feeling you would make a good pair, as Paul English did when he met Steve Hafner, his cobuilder of Kayak.com: "Steve and I are similar in many ways, but we are also very different in actual technical skill set. But we both detected a level of aggression or commitment in the other one and felt that, 'Wow, if you put two cofounders together that are this aggressive . . .'"[2]

Finally, like countless other cobuilders such as Jin Sook and Don Chang of Forever 21, Gary Erickson and Kit Crawford of Clif Bar, or Kevin and Julia Hartz of Eventbrite, maybe you already are actually married to one another.

However and whomever you met, hopefully you have gotten to know, respect, and trust the person you have chosen to build with. That relationship is the bedrock on which your business will be built. And with any luck, the relationship will survive intact and maybe even strengthen, regardless of how the venture evolves. But such a connection will take real effort and attention to the kinds of personality issues we discuss in this book.

All these cobuilder relationships are like marriage in other respects as well. The goal is more than mere compatibility. And the challenge is to base a relationship on mutual respect in pursuit of a common goal. While you may share certain capabilities and values, your skills are ideally more complementary than conflicting—and your respective decision-making prerogatives are clear. In effect, your strengths offset the weaknesses of the other person, and vice versa—the proverbial whole being greater than the sum of its parts.

Co-*What?*

The decision to cobuild invokes the counsel given in many wedding ceremonies: "This commitment should not be entered into lightly." Several factors come into play when you're considering building a venture with others. In fact, there are so many dimensions to consider, this topic could fill an entire book by itself.

Our intention here is not to give you a detailed treatise on the topic, but rather to examine the issue through the lens of Builder Types. The core question is this: Are the cobuilders truly coequals? To answer that, consider how you plan to handle four key aspects of governance and reward: splitting the ownership pie, decision making, title, and responsibility.

Here's a useful way you might think of these four dimensions, in light of the Builder Personalities involved. Remember, there is no single right solution to this builder-builder fit puzzle. Nor does resolution in one area dictate an answer in another.

Builders and their prospective cobuilders should determine whether they have the same expectations on these four dimensions and others that we will discuss later. Sadly, ambiguity or a lack of shared understanding often results in bitterness, an unstable relationship, and ultimately a fracture that destroys both value and relationships.

Divvying Up the Ownership Pie

Every business builder has to figure out how to divide the company ownership pie. Who gets what share, when, and why? How much should you reserve for future contributors? What kind of ownership structure best fits your vision for how stakeholders get rewarded? Questions like these are important to address as early and candidly as possible.

The math involved in these questions is important, obviously, but its precision and apparent objectivity mask the powerful subjective forces and feelings involved here. What is fair? Why does person A get *x* percent of the company and person B get *y* percent? What truly motivates people's best performance: stock or cash compensation, his or her title in the company, recognition, a sense of being on a great team, or something else? These are complex and highly personal issues you as a builder have to weigh, regardless of how you choose to work out the math itself. And there is no single right answer here.

There are two additional thoughts to consider. First, if you are the real animating spirit of the business, don't immediately assume it will take a fifty-fifty ownership arrangement to attract a genuine cofounder to help you launch your venture. You can invite someone else to share the headaches and decisions of being a cobuilder with as much transparency and access to information as you are comfortable with. It is quite common to bring extraordinarily talented cobuilders into a fledgling company with far less equity than 50 percent.

Second, try to avoid giving away something permanent (like ownership in your company) for something of possibly temporary value (like the early contributions of a technical or marketing cofounder who loses interest or isn't as great as you both needed this person to be). Vesting both of your ownership stakes can cure a lot of ills here, however you divide the pie. After all, it's the lasting value of each other's actual contribution to the venture's success that really matters.

Focus on the Management, Not the Math

How will cobuilders divide management roles, decision-making authority, and responsibilities to get the work done? Who decides strategically important matters? Who has the final say when a significant disagreement occurs? Who's responsible for which company activities on a day-to-day basis? The answers to these questions may not reflect—and don't need to reflect—the math of ownership shares per se.

Some cobuilding teams are true coequals—Ben Cohen and Jerry Greenfield, Bill Hewlett and Dave Packard, William Procter and James Gamble, and so on.[3] Other times, the founder decides to recognize his or her first set of followers as cofounders of the endeavor. A good example of this latter model is Alibaba, in which Jack Ma, the archetype Captain, recognized all sixteen of his friends who joined him in his small apartment in Hangzhou, China, as cofounders. But the Alibaba equity pie was not divided into seventeen equal slices.

True fifty-fifty decision-making pairings can be problematic, with or without the shared title of co-CEO. They are also fragile undertakings—despite the best intentions with which they begin. When a venture is at its earliest stages, with a wide-open future ahead, it's easy to share both excitement about what's possible and enthusiasm for the tasks ahead. But as the reality unfolds and the partners learn what success will require—the sacrifices and tough choices around strategy and people, not to mention unpredictable turns in the market and possible discoveries of one another's shortcomings—those early bonds can unravel.

These fifty-fifty relationships are the most fragile over time, as the business morphs and adapts to market circumstances and operational realities. Take a look at how the complex relationship between Gates and Allen or between Jobs and Wozniak unfolded and, to some extent, unraveled over time. But coequals can work effectively if both parties are wise and flexible enough to agree on the key elements of their collaboration. The issues that matter—decision-making and tie-breaker authority; accountability; alignment of mission, values, and cultural foundations; ownership stakes—are the same ones we'll explore later in greater detail with the more common and unequal cobuilder arrangements. But they are particularly pronounced in these fifty-fifty couples.

Choosing a Cobuilder:
Clone, Complement, or Opposite?

Fundamentally, a builder can choose a clone, a complement, or an opposite as a cobuilder. Here are three examples. At Google, Brin and Page look like a pair of comparables, each with Crusader-esque vision and Explorer-like problem-solving instincts. The Gates and Allen pairing was basically between complements, at least for a while—Gates as the Driver, get-it-done partner and Allen as the Explorer (ditto for the Jobs and Wozniak duo). But opposites can also attract. That's what happened in the creation of SoulCycle and Kayak.com.

Each combination poses different challenges and possibilities. A pair of similar types tends to magnify the same gifts and gaps of each respective type. A complementary couple can do well, if they can sort out who does what when, while a pair of opposites might get stalemated arm-wrestling with each other. In the next section, we will look at the likely patterns of collaboration and conflict various builder relationships can create.

It's All About Decision Making

As mentioned, our focus is on decision making—who calls the shots in multiparty relationships. A cobuilder partnership in which each personality pulls against the other is a recipe for failure. Tug-of-war

FIGURE 6-1

Decision-Making Role: Cobuilder Pairings

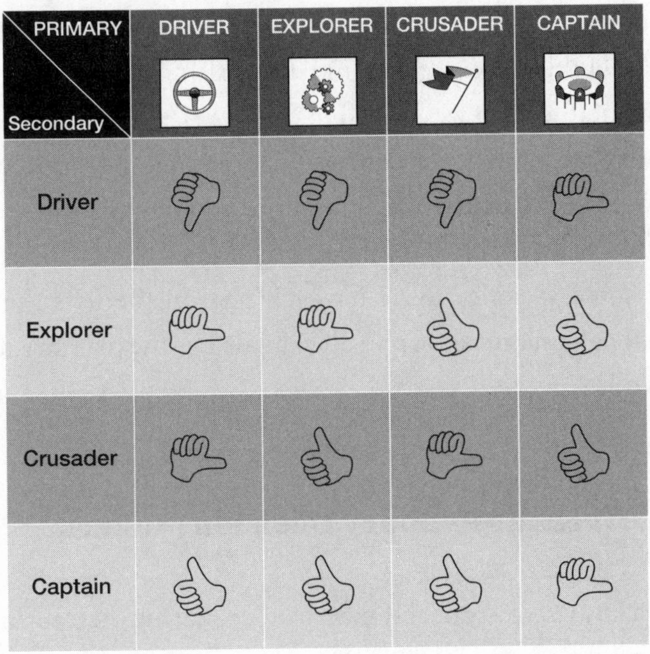

differences are often magnified throughout the organization, and schisms develop. Different employees align themselves with one cobuilder or the other, creating counterproductive intramural conflict.

While there are multiple flavors of cobuilder partnerships, figure 6-1 shows how various Builder Type pairings are likely to interact with each other across the five growth dynamics. Each axis is labeled with the primary decision-maker personality across the top and the secondary cobuilder's personality down the side. This interaction is *the* key issue—because the combination of strengths and style preferences of each personality, when combined with clear decision rights, can either draw the best out of the cobuilder or the opposite—inciting conflict.

We give a thumbs-up for synergistic pairings, a thumbs-down for problematic, conflict-prone ones, and a thumbs-sideways for cautionary ones that may need special attention. Your results may vary, but the figure points out areas worth serious, candid discussion with your prospective cobuilder. You will not find it surprising that we rate the polar complement (the term we defined in chapter 1) pairings as thumbs-up, for the very reason that the contrast in strengths and weaknesses can be the source of an effective and powerful cobuilding partnership.

Here is a brief overview of the key dynamics at play for each pairing and some specific advice for each one. In the lists that follow, the initial personality shown in all capitals has the primary decision-making role.

Drivers as Primary Decision Makers

If you're a Driver, you probably have trouble sharing the steering wheel. But as long as you occupy the primary tie-breaking role, you can benefit from joining forces with other Builder Types whose perspectives and style can smooth some of your own rougher edges. The challenge for you is whether you can allow a cobuilder to play his or her role to the maximum benefit of both of you.

- **DRIVER-Driver (thumbs-down):** This combination has high potential for conflict because Drivers are not accustomed to sharing the mantle of power. They are—by definition—driven, clear in their convictions. They have a tough time sharing decisions regarding their market-sensing gift. If you're a Driver, you prefer to direct the company from your commercial sense of how your product or service meets customer needs, while aiming to shape market development. Your personality would have a hard time as the secondary decision maker. Your focus on self can border on narcissism. Consequently, if both cofounders have this proclivity, the result can be more incendiary than synergistic. The Driver's gaps also make it difficult to pick up on soft signals of dissent or different viewpoints, whether they are from a single customer, the broader market, an employee, or an investor. A fellow Driver is not likely to offset this gap, and may exacerbate it.

- **DRIVER-Explorer (thumbs-sideways):** With this pair, success or failure lies in the allocation of decision rights. If as a Driver you can cede the non-market-facing, operational aspects of the business to your number two (an Explorer), he or she is likely to strengthen your pairing and thereby your enterprise. The Explorer's systems thinking can be highly effective in operationalizing the aspects of the business that are less interesting to many Drivers, but no less important in scaling. Likewise, the control-oriented Explorer must be comfortable in his or her role as number two, with specific spheres of influence but not necessarily the last word. Because of these caveats, we rate this combination a thumbs-sideways, with thumbs-up potential.

- **DRIVER-Crusader (thumbs-sideways):** This pair also has potential, particularly if the initial product idea came from the Driver and if the Crusader believes the value proposition has a broad mission with which he or she can inspire customers and employees alike. In this combination, each type gets to play to his or her preferences, ideally in a complementary manner. As a Driver, you tend to become so focused on the concept, market, and customer problems, you may fail to connect with and inspire your team with a sense of mission. The DRIVER-Crusader division of labor has real potential benefit. You can focus on the commercial aspects of the value proposition and market while your cobuilder Crusader uses a broader sense of mission and purpose to inspire customers and employees. Under these circumstances, Crusaders can tap another level of creativity and productivity Drivers alone are likely to miss. To make this mercenary-missionary combination work, builders need to make several nuanced tradeoffs of power and style. So we give this pair a thumbs-sideways.

- **DRIVER-Captain (thumbs-up):** This partnership is likely to work because the Driver needs a second in command who can tap the innate productivity of the team. As a Driver, you can become so completely focused on the market, customer needs, and your ideas that the rest of your team can feel unappreciated and underinspired. Captains have the finesse to read and support you and quietly do what is needed to align the troops. Because strengths can be harmonized in this combination, we give it a thumbs-up.

 Explorers as Primary Decision Makers

As long as the cobuilder brings his or her own problem-solving chops to the table, Explorers can be good matches for other Builder Types—with one exception, the Driver, who has a similarly control-oriented intensity.

- **EXPLORER-Driver (thumbs-down):** This combination has high potential for conflict because as an Explorer, you are very hands-on. In fact, some call your type *control freaks*. Drivers also have a high need to have things done their way. This common control instinct, even when decision-making roles are clear, is likely to result in conflict. As an Explorer, you may well need help in areas that are not your natural strength, such as culture and talent management. Since these are also not natural assets for Drivers, either, we give this pairing a thumbs-down.

- **EXPLORER-Explorer (thumbs-sideways):** This twin pair has both positive and negative potential. On the positive side, as an Explorer, you're likely to work well with similar-minded systems thinkers. Their structured approach provides a common vocabulary and starting point as well as a path through issues. The point of conflict is control, one of your greatest needs. If you are the leading Explorer, you will have to cede some level of control to keep your number two engaged and productive. With these conditions in place, this pairing has the potential to be thumbs-up, but we label it as thumbs-sideways, because the primary decision maker must operate against type for the relationship to succeed.

- **EXPLORER-Crusader (thumbs-up):** The builders in this unit have great potential to work well together. If you're an Explorer in the primary role, a Crusader can free you to apply your systematic thinking to the problems and opportunities with the greatest potential for driving enterprise value. Because these issues are likely to be operational and structural, they provide white space for a Crusader to imbue his or her functional vision with a higher-order mission. This softer and more empathic partner can engender more loyalty and commitment from customers and employees alike. We give this pair a thumbs-up.

- **EXPLORER-Captain (thumbs-up):** This relationship has good potential for many of the same reasons as the one above. As an Explorer, once you are convinced of someone else's competency, you're more likely to cede power—although you monitor things to ensure your delegation was well founded. The Captain, like the Explorer, is an operator, but in different ways. The Captain's gifts are to operationalize through people, deploying and empowering the right ones for each role and responsibility. As an Explorer, you are motivated to figure out the gnarly problem and operationalize the solution. This team has good potential and consequently is a thumbs-up.

Crusaders as Primary Decision Makers

Crusaders, like Drivers, probably benefit most from pairing up with another builder, however for different reasons. If you're a Crusader, you might, with the right match, link your lofty vision with the operational practicalities of making it happen. The question is whether your vision is flexible enough to accommodate the different leadership and management approaches of another Builder Personality working side by side with you.

- **CRUSADER-Driver (thumbs-down):** The styles of these two Builder Types can actually be quite complementary (as we saw in the DRIVER-Crusader partnership above). However, this power allocation is not likely to prove productive. As a Crusader, you're likely to start from a position of empathy, motivating followers and customers through your mission-centered sense of purpose. This position opens up a vulnerability in which your sensitivity can sometimes overwhelm your rationality—leading you to avoid the tough decisions growth requires. In theory, a Driver should be a good complement. However, Crusaders' sensitivity and compassion can be disorienting to Drivers, who tend not to be tuned into these dimensions. Rather, the Driver applies all his or her cycles to market sensing and ideation. This pairing is likely to be a thumbs-down near miss.

- **CRUSADER-Explorer (thumbs-up):** With its complementary skills, this combo has great potential. To tap the strengths of this team, the builders need to work out the style differences early. As a Crusader, you have a penchant for being outward-facing and focused on the big-picture mission of the organization. This outlook creates a strong need for a key lieutenant to focus on the operational aspects of the enterprise. The potential point of friction stems from your type's underlying philosophy about people and the corresponding style of leadership. You are deeply empathetic and sometimes almost too trusting of those you believe are good people. The Explorer tends to build trust more through his or her head rather than heart and is focused on competency. These differing approaches ideally are combined, but run the risk that each of you will select followers in your own mold and create a balkanized culture. Conversely, if you both recognize this possible conflict and manage it deliberately, there is great potential in this pairing, so we give it a thumbs-up.

- **CRUSADER-Crusader (thumbs-sideways):** This pair runs the risk of not having either person focused on the detailed operational aspects of the business. As a Crusader, you are a big-picture thinker, and as such, you can benefit from a more detail-oriented and exacting partner in the second chair. If you can hire this more operationally focused counterpart on your team, great things are possible. Otherwise, this high-minded pairing is less likely to really scale their business. For this reason, we rate it a thumbs-sideways.

- **CRUSADER-Captain (thumbs-up):** Builders in this team work well together. As a Crusader, you need an operator, and the Captain can fill that role. You and a Captain are both very focused on people—you through your empathy and ability to give employees a sense of mission, and the Captain through his or her belief that the right person in the right job taps an inner potential for productivity and purpose. This philosophical alignment with role clarity earns a thumbs-up.

Captains as Primary Decision Makers

If you're a Captain, you can be the most compatible cobuilder of our quartet—not surprising, given your comfort with collaboration and consensus building. But your *we*-versus-*me*-based leadership style should not be confused with the lack of a clear agenda. As a Captain, you are often focused more on getting your colleagues aligned around that agenda than on participating in group decisions. That's why we give you a mixed scorecard below.

- **CAPTAIN-Driver (thumbs-sideways):** This pair has the potential to be thumbs-up if the Driver is young and otherwise willing to suspend his or her natural drive in favor of being a student of the game. As a Captain, you are the most natural leader in figuring out how to tap the motivations of team members to get the very best out of each. You may just be able to provide the sense of shared ownership many Drivers crave to create and achieve marketplace impact. Since as a Captain you tend to delegate operational details to others, you're likely to hand over issues of commercialization to a Driver lieutenant and allow this person to run with it. Conversely, if the Driver is of roughly your same age and experience, this pairing can be fraught with problems.

As a Captain, you are likely to expect your number two to operate with the principle of people first and team empowerment, neither of which is the Driver's natural proclivity. So we see this as a thumbs-sideways situation.

- **CAPTAIN-Explorer (thumbs-up):** Like the EXPLORER-Captain pair, this team has good potential because of complementary preferences. If you're a Captain, you have an artful way to tap the expertise of others and tend to operate above the day-to-day issues. These tendencies play to the strengths of the Explorer, who likes to control the operation with his or her tools of systems thinking and facts. The challenge in this pairing, if there is one, relates to how each of you regards your employees. As a Captain, you are all about empowerment, while the Explorer tends to maintain tight boundaries around the roles of others to ensure compliance with the system. Working with an Explorer, you can get a strong operational lieutenant and, ideally, can teach your cobuilder how to unleash even greater potential of others through looser boundaries and the empowerment than can flow from that. We give this pair a thumbs-up.

- **CAPTAIN-Crusader (thumbs-up):** This combination has strong potential for the same reason the preceding pair has: complementarity. As a Captain, you are comfortable ceding power to the strengths of your lieutenants. Here, you can get the mission-based loft a Crusader brings to the business, yet not fall victim to your partner's operational weaknesses, because you can deploy others against this important set of responsibilities. This relationship gets a thumbs-up.

- **CAPTAIN-Captain (thumbs-sideways):** Here we see the potential for conflict under the logic that too much homogeneity allows weaknesses to multiply. Unlike some of the other twin pairs, this one is potentially problematic but not for reasons of personal conflict. Rather, as a Captain, you tend to solve the problems directly in front of you and may not have the wider, longer view of the other types. A double-Captain team could miss a shift in the marketplace, particularly likely in fast-moving industries like technology. This potential for a lethal surprise leads us to rate this pair a thumbs-sideways.

The bottom line on these tandem builder arrangements is this: anytime you put two strong-willed, ambitious, and confident individuals together, you can expect fireworks. Cobuilder pairings can work wonderfully, as long as the decision-making rights and areas of primary responsibility are clear, both for the individuals and to the organization the builders are leading. Forming those arrangements with a better insight into the underlying personality pluses and minuses of the two Builder Types should make that conversation and negotiation more productive.

1 + 1 Is Addition, but 1 + 2 Is Multiplication

There are many combinations and permutations of cobuilder relationships, from two-person arrangements to multiparty teams like those that founded Warby Parker and Pinterest. And sometimes, several enthusiastic cofounders remain tethered together only for a short time, leaving one or two members of the initial band to stick with the venture after the others lose interest once the rigors of business building become clear.

Our experience and research suggest that the complexities multiply rather than simply add for every additional individual involved. But the inclusion of other people might also make it easier to avoid irreconcilable standoffs. So don't rule out that possibility if a threesome or "more-some" intrigues you. And remember our advice about vesting curing many sins.

A Trio Starts at Airbnb

Two designers and an engineer walk into a bar . . . well, actually, the meeting took place elsewhere, but out of those early discussions about rethinking the entire hotel and couch-surfing experience came an idea to democratize it. With Driver Joe Gebbia and Crusader Brian Chesky on the guest and host experience and design side, and Explorer Nathan Blecharczyk handling engineering, Airbnb opened up a new world of private apartments and homes to visitors worldwide.

"It's pretty unusual, and I actually attribute a lot of our success to that combination," Blecharczyk says. "We see things very differently because of our backgrounds and we've discovered that's an asset. Sometimes it takes a little longer to reconcile our perspectives, but we find if we take the time to do that we can come up with a superior solution. One that takes into account both points of view."[4]

However many individuals you are considering as cobuilders, we suggest you focus on the basic building unit here: two individuals and their personalities. If you can solve the chemistry of that collaboration, you might be ready to tackle the higher math of trios, quartets, and beyond.

What to Do Next

If you're a builder considering beginning a cobuilder relationship, we suggest you first take a careful look at what kind of arrangement you want (the "co-what?" question). Then explore each other's motivations, decision-making patterns, and leadership and management style.

If both of you haven't yet discovered your precise Builder Personality, you might start by visiting our www.builtforgrowth.com website to do that. Then you can sit down with your counterpart to compare notes on how your types might complement, match, or conflict with one another, and see if there is a meeting of the minds on how to handle those situations. These issues are good places to start a more productive discussion—a kind of builders' prenuptial, if you like—to get the best of your mutual aspirations as you build this venture together.

Conversation First, Negotiation Later

Too often, advisers jump to the view that the aforementioned issues are necessarily matters for negotiation, often with lawyers involved. This viewpoint almost inevitably assumes, and sometimes even creates, an adversarial arm-wrestling posture for both parties. It also may miss the possibility of more genuine conversation around these issues—a conversation that produces a clearer understanding of what's really important to each individual.

For example, you might assume questions such as title and compensation, both obviously important issues to settle, matter equally to both of you. Often, that assumption is not correct; one person may care far more about being in charge of customer-facing marketing or sales, while the other really enjoys running things behind the scenes or being in charge of design or engineering.

We suggest a slightly different way to get these issues on the table for discussion and handshake resolution before you call in the attorneys. It's an old-fashioned approach: face-to-face conversation with deep listening and reflection from both players.

If you're prepared to try this first, you may be pleasantly surprised to discover your areas of agreement and accommodation are much larger than the zones of disagreement that will require some frank, tough negotiation between you. Here's a starting list of the issues you should discuss, framed as questions worthy of back-and-forth discussion:[5]

- What's your real vision for where this company should go, by when?

- What's important to you about that vision and time frame?

- What matters most to you in our working to fulfill that vision: money, public recognition, personal pride, freedom to do this our way, or something else?

- What situations do you think best bring out our respective strengths, and which expose our weaknesses? What's your thinking behind that?

- What do you think each of us is looking for in this business?

- How do you think we should agree to handle things when we disagree?

- What's your biggest fear or worry about what lies ahead for our business?

These questions don't read like the usual checklist for a buy-sell agreement between partners or a laundry list for a prenuptial agreement. This list is different because we want to encourage you to explore some of these deeper-level matters that tie more directly and importantly to who you are as individuals first. Your personalities will manifest themselves inevitably as you go along, so you'll be better off if you understand one another's makeup sooner rather than later.

There will be many other issues to handle, several of which will probably require legal help. And remember, lawyers are very good at memorializing agreements already struck by their clients; attorneys do not always have to wear their negotiating hats to be effective advisers. Direct conversations between you and your prospective cobuilder can, at the very least, narrow the range of issues for which you'll need outside counsel before you get too far along in the building process.

And yes, it's probably a good idea to put it down in writing with the help of an experienced attorney. We've seen too many handshake understandings evaporate in the aftermath of imperfect memory, not to mention the antipathy that may arise from builder pairings gone awry.

We'll leave the final words of advice here to Guy Kawasaki, who nicely captures the essence of what a great cobuilder relationship needs to have: "Some people like to sweat the details (microscopes). Others like to ignore the details and worry about the big issues (telescopes). A successful startup needs both types of founders to succeed (gyroscopes)."[6]

7

RECRUITING YOUR INSIDE TEAM

Selecting the People Who Work Best with You

Builders who try to build alone build little. Your prodigious talents are best unleashed when you combine yours with those of other individuals. Their perspective, skill, and commitment can create a force multiplier for your own distinctive personality characteristics.

If you're a builder, you need a crew—whether they're called employees, teammates, associates, or colleagues. You depend on the talent and dedication of other individuals, from the early days before launch to later stages of scaling a successful business. And as we suggested in our description of the team growth dynamic (i.e., galvanizing individual talent for collaborative impact; see chapter 2), you will face these talent-matching challenges in unpredictable and recurring ways. This chapter focuses on how you can develop, implement, and then institutionalize a talent-recruiting strategy based on the chemistry between you and the individuals you will need as you build for growth.

In our experience, the most effective builders of growth choose their core team as carefully as they think about product, customers and investors; and some, even more so. They then hold their team of direct reports to the same standard for their respective hires, who in turn do the same across the organization, so that the same talent DNA is replicated throughout the company. One way to accomplish this goal is to ask prospective team members three key questions (beyond their functional skill competency) that can help you decide if there is a likely fit between the person and your organization.

1. **What are the candidate's motivations and career priorities?** Does the person think of work as just a job to pay the bills and support a lifestyle, while the individual's real fulfillment lies in other non-work activities? Or does the candidate see the job as an expression of who he or she is, so that it defines an important part of the person's meaning in life?

2. **What kind of work setting and culture brings out his or her best?** Is he or she most comfortable working with very clear, specific direction? Or does he or she do best in a more open and free-form environment? Does the candidate prefer to work closely with other colleagues in an environment with a strong team culture? Or does he or she do best as an individual contributor? Does the person operate best in a nurturing, learning, and relationship-based environment or in an expert, demanding, and transactional one?

3. **Where is the person in the arc of his or her career?** Is the candidate at the beginning of a career, seeking an opportunity to learn, or later in a career and hoping to apply hard-earned knowledge and experience? If the former, is he or she flexible in approach and style, that is, perhaps an ideal apprentice? If so, then you

must ask yourself whether your culture is committed and staffed to train. Conversely, if the candidate is in the later stages of a career, the issue of fit with the builder's style is vitally important, particularly for more senior roles. Although the ideal pairings of senior team member and Builder Type can be highly productive for both, misfires here are costly.

With these screening questions in mind, along with each builder's style and preferences, let's see how each Builder Personality can select the crew members with whom the builder is most likely to work effectively.

 ## The Driver's Manual:
Tell Your Team to Fasten Their Seatbelts!

Drivers drive! If you're a Driver, your intensity is grounded in your confidence that the products and services you're bringing to the market are exactly what the market needs (even if sometimes it hasn't been looking for them). You see market acceptance almost as a form of personal validation. Your expectation of perfection is not a great fit for some team members, while others find it inspiring.

Drivers expect a lot from their followers. Like a demanding coach who pushes his or her team to redouble their practice intensity or yells at a player on the sidelines for missing an assignment on the court, you can be a harsh taskmaster. Sometimes that rough style can yield victories worth the pain and embarrassment along the way. But your team members can't expect a lot of TLC with you as their business builder.

Working with and for Drivers often takes something that probably doesn't show up on most candidates' résumés: a very thick skin. As a Driver, you can be particularly tough on the people around you. Your single-mindedness can compromise your sensitivity to others' feelings and pride. You may have already been surprised when you lost a valued colleague who left because of a bruised ego.

A Driver's organization may not be the best place to work for someone who considers work just a job, deriving deeper life satisfaction outside the workplace. As a Driver, you often expect everyone to be as driven and perfectionistic as you are. You run a tight ship, with exacting performance expectations. This environment tends to fit those who see themselves as experts and are comfortable working as individual contributors. Your best team members may be on either end of their career arc—more-senior people accustomed to this kind of culture or apprentices willing to work in a demanding environment as the price of learning new skills they desire.

As a Driver, you tend not to be focused on ensuring an open, collaborative, and flexible culture in your organization. In your impatient search for results and accountability, you tend to ignore usual chains of command—a habit that can catch your lieutenants off guard. You may allow an implicit hierarchy to develop according to expertise, impact, and drive, with those who demonstrate all three becoming elevated both formally and informally within the organization.

Your most valuable followers are those who have earned your trust by meeting your tough expectations across initiatives and over time. Perhaps those individuals have contributed something unique to your company's market understanding, product differentiation, or both.

While not necessarily admitting it even to yourself, you may view most other followers as dispensable resources rather than genuine collaborators in a shared endeavor. You are likely to have the "what have you done for me lately?" question in the back of your mind in dealing with rank-and-file employees. So figure out how you define and measure success in ways potential team members can understand. Is it sales, profits, growth, market share, or valuation relative to competitors? Or is it industry recognition, personal wealth, or some other metric?

While every builder wants success, Drivers crave it. You can be abrupt and impatient when faced with performance results that don't match your ambitions. However, if your team members can stand, or maybe even enjoy, the sometimes white-hot intensity that comes from working close to your preferred metrics, they may earn a seat in your vehicle . . . and maybe even ride shotgun.

The Explorer's Lab:
Assembling the Right Crew to Crack the Next Code

As an Explorer, you prefer employees who share your practical curiosity and commitment to finding commercially viable, clever solutions to big customer problems. But you can get bored with the more routine aspects of your company's operations, however necessary they may be to the success of the business. So what kind of crew might fit your personality best?

As with the Driver, your organization is not ideally suited for the it's-just-a-job view of employment. Explorers have high expectations, and your systems thinking pervades almost every interaction. This cultural expectation translates into a work environment more suited to team members who derive their life satisfaction from work. Because cracking the code is everything to you as an Explorer, you can create exciting team and individual contributor cultures, but they tend not be all that nurturing.

Expertise and knowledge reign supreme. So this is not an ideal place for an apprentice, unless he or she is willing to be a dutiful student, learns quickly, and has a tough skin when it comes to inevitable rookie mistakes. Senior functional experts, on the other hand, represent ideal members of your team, as they can provide support in key areas that don't interest you but which are key to scaling the enterprise.

You need a crew comfortable with tough intellectual competition. Because you don't suffer fools lightly, your people need to show their stuff to establish credibility in their domain. Solutions count—they're the currency of your realm.

You don't want team members to be your clones. You will need, if not always appreciate, analytical creativity and tenacity from other disciplinary backgrounds as your enterprise grows. In fact, team members skilled in areas outside your own personal interest zone—perhaps like HR, supply-chain management, or finance—may get far more freedom working in your organization. That can translate into a wonderful recruiting tool for you to bring exceptional talent onto your team in those domains.

If you really need to master one of these areas in your company for your own comfort level, fine. But beware—your questioning can come across as second-guessing and eroding the esprit de corps and mutual accountability that are the hallmarks of highly functioning teams.

Regardless of your own prowess as an Explorer, you need others' skill sets to fully realize the potential of the product, technology, and service solutions you and your core team of puzzle solvers have developed. Sometimes the growth of your business will depend more on people who can replicate the solution you've already produced than on colleagues who can help you solve the next puzzle. And look for team members who can keep things moving, pay the bills, deal with the staff, make deliveries on time, and keep customers happy. This will free you up to stay focused on cracking the next code.

Crusaders Need Intrepid Missionaries:
Sharing and Carrying Your Flag

If you're a Crusader, you're a big-picture leader. You focus on the overarching mission of your organization and want employees aligned with that higher-order agenda. Second only to your Captain cousins, you pride yourself on the loyal band of followers you've attracted to your cause. But as a Crusader, you need more than just loyal followers. You also need functional experts to operationalize and scale your mission—team members who are well into the arc of their careers, especially in areas like finance, operations, or HR, which may not be your natural sweet spot.

You need people around you who have the tenacity and dedication worthy of the crusade you are leading. That means looking for individuals willing to invest more than just time in their job. Ideal team members for a Crusader see their work as a part of how they define themselves; they are fully bought into your firm's vision for impact. These employees must be able to thrive in the kind of free-form work environments you often prefer—reinforced by your belief in nurturing individuals, working together, and learning through personal relationships with one another.

Your ideal candidate's motivation for joining forces with you should be the appeal of your crusade. However, they should also be comfortable with a fair amount of ambiguity, while having a strong do-it-yourself initiative.

As a Crusader, you may be vulnerable to a hiring pitfall we have noticed with many of your Builder Personality Type. Crusaders can mistake personal loyalty and commitment to the mission for competency. If you are a Crusader hiring for a skill-intensive discipline, get input and support from a board member or another expert who can probe each candidate on the technical competency required for the position.

Your team members may find themselves frustrated from time to time with your difficulty in translating their genuine zeal into the day-to-day details necessary to achieve the core mission you share. Sometimes, a solution to this frustration is as basic as working backward from the mission statement and showing how your team's everyday activities can noticeably improve or accelerate this goal. In other words, show your team members how they can wrap themselves in the flag of your business. Other times, it may require the more detailed kind of operational planning any team needs.

Be prepared to press the flesh with your new recruits, and remind your veterans of how important their work is to the cause and business you champion. They need to feel they're sharing, if not carrying, the same flag as you. If you are a Crusader, your employees can feel at times that working for you is a wild ride, but your gut instinct or vision is also probably one reason they signed up for your crusade in the first place.

Getting Your Captain Signals Straight:
In the Huddle and on the Field

People tapped by a Captain to join a team are fortunate. As a Captain, you are by nature comfortable with, and committed to, positive team dynamics in building your venture. But like any Captain committed to phenomenal results, you demand performance across the team that matches your expectations. You challenge as well as motivate and support players on your teams. This means you are capable of working well with team members at various places in their careers: eager apprentices, people seeking a leader role model, or people further along in their careers, seeking the ideal assignment to apply their skills.

Given your team focus, Captain-led businesses are arguably the best developers of talent across functions and tenure. While you may tolerate more free-form cultures and styles, make sure your colleagues do not mistake what appears to be greater flexibility for a lack of accountability and role clarity. These two tools—accountability and role clarity—are among the sharpest in your kit, and you tend to use them swiftly in removing underperformers.

You recruit for and expect collaboration in both servicing the customer and advancing the company's interest. In return, you create supportive environments in which individuals can learn and continually improve.

Morale matters to you, as does culture. Reconciling your team ethic with your high-results expectations is a continuing challenge for both you and your team. The phrase "iron fist in the velvet glove" comes close to capturing these two sides of your approach to leadership.

As a Captain, you are not looking for groupthink or some campfire Kumbaya bond with your team members; you just seek an effective way to harmonize and leverage their collective capabilities to go after the challenge ahead. This balancing of the nurturing side with high expectations helps you hold team members personally accountable for their results.

You are probably the best listener among our builder quartet. For this reason, members of your crew are more likely to have their opinions and ideas solicited and heard. Hopefully, they will take advantage of that open door.

We call your type of builder a Captain, because you are on the field with the rest of your team. You're a bit more like a player-coach—deciding plays, making substitutions, sizing up the game, shoring up morale, but also running plays in real time. Working in this kind of setting can be exhilarating for your team members because of the opportunity and visibility that can come from interacting with such an engaged builder.

But you need to reinforce the message that their invitation to your Captain's huddle is easily revocable if their prowess on the field declines noticeably. Your message is clear—nothing personal, just keep doing your job!

Talent Management for All Builder Types

Of course there are other factors at play for certain positions you will fill in building and scaling your company. The following advice pertains to an overarching talent management strategy.

- As we indicated above, as a Driver or an Explorer, you can be a good mentor for like-minded young talent wired similarly to you and committed to work through your high expectations and blunt feedback to become more skilled. As you scale your business, the key question is whether you hire and reward your management team to do the same and to instill this form of mentorship as a core value of your company. We have seen many examples of companies that mentor and those that do not, but those who make mentoring a key priority tend to scale more easily.

- Crusaders often create supportive, collaborative learning environments, which can be ideal for growing young talent. That said, the deep competency and commitment to mentoring within each discipline must be in place for you to realize your dream of being a learning environment.

- As mentioned above, as a Captain, you are likely to create an environment in which both young and more senior, experienced managers can thrive. You are adept at placing people in positions that stretch them, but not to the breaking point. Consequently, your management team has probably taken on this skill and builds talent from within. Although you may use a velvet glove when recruiting and nurturing talent, make sure prospective candidates know your supportive approach is anchored in a strong emphasis on accountability.

Figure 7-1 depicts the most likely successful matches between your particular personality and job candidates on the dimensions of motivation, work setting and culture preference, and career stage with which we started this chapter.

FIGURE 7-1

Candidate and Builder Type Alignment

BUILDER TYPE / Candidate Characteristics	DRIVER	EXPLORER	CRUSADER	CAPTAIN
Job Expectation Just a job				✓
Defines who person is	✓	✓	✓	✓
Work Setting and Culture Tight	✓	✓		
Free-form			✓	✓
Team-Based Style Individual contributor	✓	✓	✓	
Nurturing, relationship-based			✓	✓
Demanding, transactional-based	✓	✓		
Career Arc* Early apprentice	✓ (If OK with culture and style)	✓ (If OK with culture and style)	✓	✓
Senior, established	✓	✓	✓	✓

*We chose to focus on the early and later stages of a candidate's career arc. Alignment is especially important at the beginning of a career, when developing one's personal repertoire of skills and style, and when as a builder, you probably have a greater chance to mold this repertoire. Later on, a candidate presumably has more choice in selecting where to apply his or her skills and therefore can be more demanding in finding the right alignment with you.

Too many ventures fail not because they have bad products, lousy business models, too little money, or uninterested customers, but because they don't get the team dynamics and work culture right. As a builder, you may do a great job of selling and telling to get your businesses off the ground, but then flunk at gelling—developing an effective, high-performing team of talented people to grow that business to the scale worthy of its potential. Armed with the insights in this chapter, you can improve your odds of achieving what may be the most important fit of all: that between your Builder Personality and the team members you choose—and who, in turn, choose you—to build this business.

8

ATTRACTING YOUR BEST FINANCIAL SPONSORS

Powering Vision with the Right Capital

How important is Builder Personality to the financial sponsors of startups? Here's how Paul Maeder, managing director of Highland Capital Partners and former chairman of the National Venture Capital Association, puts it: "The builder's personality type tells me what to look for . . . It is just about everything. I don't invest in companies. I invest in people's careers."[1]

In this chapter, we will look at how you might attract, select, and collaborate with the best investors (if you're building a stand-alone startup) or the best executive sponsor (if you're building a new corporate venture) for your Builder Personality Type. The central challenge in both situations is how you can find the backer whose strategic mandate and investor style preferences best mesh with your own.

Financial sponsors (aka investors) of new ventures differ as to whether product, market size, the fit between the two, timing, or some other set of intuitive factors is the single most important element to a new venture's success. However, virtually all investors agree the personal makeup of the builder and chemistry between builder and crew are among the most important factors they consider when deciding to invest, and most outside investors we spoke with claim the builder him or herself is the focus of their most intense examination.

Given these responses, we find it more than a little curious that few if any academics, pundits in the entrepreneurial arena, or other observers have spent more time systematically examining the central question of Builder Personality. Without a rigorous, proven methodology for characterizing and identifying the different types of successful builders, up to this point we have been left with only anecdotes as guides. However, our Personality-Based Clustering technique (see Appendix A) has now provided a framework for examining how the motivations, preferences, and behaviors of each personality directly affect how different types of builders build for growth.

By understanding your Builder Personality, you can more deliberately evaluate your fit with prospective investors, and vice versa. In our experience, certain investors' mandate and preferences work more or less effectively with each personality. Using our Builder Personality Discovery tool, both you and your prospective backers can better decide whether to join forces. Experienced investors know they must create a bond of trust with the builders and crews in whom they invest. That makes both common and financial sense. After all, product–market fit can be thwarted when builders and backers lack a good fit.

In the following pages, we look at each Builder Personality profile as a potential match with independent investors like venture-capital or private-equity firms, as well as corporate executive backers of inside ventures. But first, a word about the different funding environment between independent and corporate startups.

Sponsors of Independent and Corporate Builders:
Kindred Spirits but Not Identical Twins

Investors in independent builders and their corporate executive counterparts share the imperative for growth. But each financial backer plays its role differently. Venture capital firms, angels, and private-equity investors usually put money into independent earlier-stage ventures, seeking to capitalize on opportunities ignored or mishandled by established companies. Their C-suite counterparts sponsor employee builders to launch new businesses from the inside or, in some cases, to buy later-stage companies created by entrepreneurial builders.

Both corporate and independent venture building satisfy Harvard Business School professor Howard Stevenson's definition of entrepreneurship: "pursuing opportunity beyond the resources under control." But corporate entrepreneurs—unlike their independent counterparts—have to worry about strategic alignment with their company. They must access budget, staff, and other resources currently committed to existing activities or markets and redesign decision making, management systems, and team culture to mirror the nimbler and informal requirements for launching any new venture.

If you're a builder inside a corporation, the good news is you already have what your outside counterparts spend an enormous amount of effort seeking: potential funding and access to resources, technology, facilities, talent, and even customers. But too often, those resources can often feel like mere window displays to a sidewalk shopper—nice to imagine, but hard to obtain. The corporate builder must learn to tap these resources by building alliances with those who control them across the organization.

However, if you are an inside builder, your potential sponsors operate within different parameters than do their venture capitalist counterparts. External sponsors tend to focus on whether there's a clear path to a big and rapid exit, since their key metric is internal rate of return (IRR), which is highly sensitive to the time their capital is invested. While the venture capitalist has a portfolio of investments and expects more than 10 percent of them to result in a total loss of capital, corporate backers operate within tighter constraints.

Corporate sponsors evaluate investing in internal ventures through the lens of their company's cost of capital and return on investment. Their focus on value creation and value capture usually relates to a venture's potential impact on earnings, growth, or both, rather than a profitable exit. And this usually means that new ventures inside big companies have to offer much larger scale possibilities than many of their outside counterparts, simply to register on the host's financial radar.

They are also playing a longer game, even while they and you may have to show accelerated returns to an impatient public market or investor group. When a corporate sponsor is acquiring an independent venture, the sponsor (and you, if you are the one selling) has to worry whether the acquisition will fit strategically and culturally into the company's milieu, capabilities, and customer network. And many acquisitions, if not most, do not.

With that background, let's see how your Builder Personality might best match with prospective investors.

 ## Fueling the Driver:
Finding Capital with the Right Octane

The best sponsor for a Driver is focused on product–market fit. Some investors see that fit as the magical ingredient and don't particularly care which kind of builder can show it to them. Andy Rachleff, co-founder of Benchmark Capital, a famous Silicon Valley venture firm, puts it this way: "In technology, I believe success is almost exclusively a function of whether or not the company finds product–market fit. And it's not at all an issue of perseverance, or hard work, or personality. If you have the right product–market fit, you could be the world's worst executive and still succeed in a very big way. How else can you explain twenty-four-year-olds running billion-dollar companies? Personality archetypes, to me, don't matter very much."[2]

If you're a Driver, this emphasis on product–market fit favors you. You tend to do well with outside investors like Rachleff, given their focus on the product solution you so confidently tout—provided you can back it up with traction in the market. The ideal investor partner with your personality strikes a careful balance between excitement for your product vision and not "going native" and thereby losing objectivity. You need your investor to remain objective about the current level of market development and the maturity of both your product line and the market it addresses.

Your passion for your solution is great, but it can lead to overreaching when it comes to negotiating a fair valuation, especially in your venture's early stages. A seasoned investor can help you develop a more realistic view of market maturity and corresponding valuation. This smarter view can enable both of you to align expectations, so invested capital, valuation, and product–market fit are more in synch.

If you're a Driver inside an existing corporation, you face three challenges. The first is whether your host company is the right kind of sponsor for the business you're pursuing. There may simply be no match between the strategic interests, or resources, of your firm and your idea. Most corporations are not in the business of making venture-capital-style investments without strategic alignment.

If there is a persuasive, or at least plausible, case to be made that your proposed new venture does align with your company's vision, you face a second hurdle: how can this investment be structured to provide the right level and timing of financial support, while also providing you and your crew with the kind of compensation rewards you want for undertaking the endeavor?

With respect to negotiating a reward structure that motivates you and your team, you may fall prey to rigid policies and lack of precedents within your company, unless your firm has had experience designing investment and compensation frameworks for other insider-led ventures. In fact, you may be more willing than your other three builder counterparts to share the risks of your ideas with your corporate sponsor. So be ready to suggest novel arrangements and even new business models that might mitigate your firm's risks while offering you higher compensation in exchange for your taking on more risk and achieving predetermined milestones. For example, phantom stock, spin-outs, a negotiated buyback option in exchange for allowing your new venture to take root outside the company—these are examples of the kind of flexibility your company needs to motivate and keep an ambitious Driver and his or her team in the organization.

Third, both you and your potential sponsors need to agree that a personality like yours can successfully launch a scalable business with or within a company like theirs. Why? As a Driver, you are probably the spikiest of the four Builder Types, and those sharp edges can be a challenge inside a corporate environment. Your personality is often easy to spot, precisely because your brusqueness, intense ambition, and obvious self-confidence may stand out from your softer-edged colleagues.

A corporate sponsor supporting you as a Driver may also need to decide whether he or she is willing to get out of your way, so both of you can see whether your idea is likely to pan out as successfully as promised. You have your own firm ideas of what it's going to take to bring your notion to market, including the kinds of people you want involved. You're unlikely to appreciate suggestions that you hire colleagues who do not fit the operating intensity you envision in your venture.

Your Builder Personality is also arguably the least suited to be lashed to the rest of the corporate infrastructure—budgeting procedures, meeting protocols, IT system specs, and HR hiring and compensation policies. Your sponsor needs to open up the road a bit for Drivers like you, but must also be prepared to deal with ruffled feathers left in your exhaust. You can be disrupters in both a positive and negative sense, so expect your inside sponsor to keep an eye on that balance for both your sakes. Your ideal internal sponsor buffers the corporation from you and does a bit of the reverse, but is careful not to put a governor on your engine. After all, the sponsoring company may need precisely your personality to achieve market-changing impact.

Indeed, truly entrepreneurial Drivers may be harder to find inside existing corporations in the first place. They are often the first people to leave a large company after having failed to convince their firms to embrace their ideas. Keep in mind, however, the track record of the marriage between corporate Drivers and their employers is not exactly encouraging, as a recent Accenture global study on corporate entrepreneurship found: "Three-fourths of large companies feel that their employees are sufficiently entrepreneurial; yet, of all the entrepreneurs who worked in a large company previously, 75 percent left because they felt that they could not be entrepreneurial within the corporate setting."

The examples of these problematic relationships are legion: from members of the Traitorous Eight, who left Fairchild Semiconductor and then spawned the high-tech innovation explosion that became Silicon Valley, to Mark Cuban, who was fired from his first two corporate jobs, never to return to working for anyone but himself. Some corporate Drivers, when paired with the right sponsor, can unleash their commercial gifts inside a large enterprise. However, many cannot and leave to build on their own, often selling their creations to a large company that was unable to foster disruptive growth from within. For corporate sponsors and other members of the C-suite, we see this as a bit of a cautionary tale, because acquisition is far more expensive than accommodating the aggressive nature of a Driver who builds breakaway value.

Chartering the Explorer:
Engineering the Right Fit

Explorers are often drawn to investors who share their systems thinking. If you're an Explorer, your focus on solving challenging problems by creating systematic, carefully engineered solutions can be an excellent fit for venture firms composed of partners with engineering backgrounds. Drawn in by how well your personality can describe the intricacies of the problem and the completeness by which your solution addresses it, investors can create a geek fest in early meetings with Explorers like you.

The question of your motivation can catch some investors by surprise. For many Explorers, money—after a certain point—is not all that motivating. But compensation in the form of cash and equity is one of only two financial tools outside investors have to motivate builders and their teams.

It turns out the other tool, investment capital, can be more motivating to Explorers. As an Explorer, you want to move your ingenious solution from product to portfolio to platform, and doing so requires the right steadfast capital partner. Your ideal partner shares your voracious curiosity and accompanying appetite for commercializing systematic solutions. Access to supportive capital to continue inventing can be far more appealing to an Explorer who's playing for a higher-order goal—market impact and perhaps industry transformation.

If you're an Explorer working in an existing company, are you focused on solving a challenge that's strategically significant for your company? This question is not about your intellectual prowess. You have the same systems-thinking, disciplined yet creative minds we've already seen in your independent entrepreneurial counterparts like Brian Coester, Tom Phillips, and Mark Bonfigli, among others.

But savvy corporate sponsors know not every problem is strategically valuable, and not every great problem solver makes a great business builder. It's not as easy as simply pulling people out of the engineering department or lab and assuming they can be turned into overnight entrepreneurs. Scientists, technologists, and engineers may all be great at the discovery process, but they often lack the skills to commercialize their own ideas. That's probably one reason why less than 1 percent of the inventions patented in the United States ever make money. And your company's growth agenda is too important to be left to amateurs.

So if you are a corporate Explorer, you and your potential sponsor might be better off thinking like a Captain, assembling a team of complementary players who can leverage and commercialize your proposed solution. After all, you probably don't have to worry about the kinds of divide-the-pie controversies and recruiting challenges that many outside entrepreneurs face. Some of the people you need may already work for the company; management can decide what they work on and with whom—and you can be the beneficiary.

This access to inside colleagues can help you realize the commercial value of your own idea. Norbert Berta, the Explorer behind Johnson & Johnson's invention of the caplet dosage form, which was key to the Tylenol brand recovery, needed his colleagues' capabilities to capture its value. So consider the kinds of talent necessary to successfully marshal a new venture through the five growth dynamics, and don't be reluctant to seek and accept other insiders who can help. But be wary of accepting your sponsor's suggestions too quickly. You may well want and need the freedom to hire your analytical peers from outside.

As with any new venture within or even outside an existing company, cultural conflicts are likely to develop. Explorers tend not to be too focused on the softer sides of the enterprises they build. But culture is likely to be particularly important to your sponsor and your company. So be on the lookout for early signs of tension and possible schisms in this area. It's not that your sponsor necessarily expects your venture to be a clone of the existing business, but you do need to make sure to reflect the core values on which your company is based and by which the customers know it.

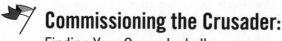 Commissioning the Crusader:
Finding Your Queen Isabella

If you are a Crusader, your ideal financial sponsor is someone whose horizon matches your own vision, with the temperament and patient capital to boot. You need investors whose role is more like the one Queen Isabella played for Christopher Columbus than the rapacious one Gordon Gekko displayed with his portfolio companies in the movie *Wall Street*. In other words, you want a sponsor more interested in long-term development than in short-term profit. To some extent, there is always tension between an early-stage venture capitalist's desire for a timely exit and a founder's quest to build a long-term, successful enterprise that grows well after the early supporters have cashed out. But that tension can be especially acute with Crusader-led ventures.

Investors experienced in funding Crusaders are well aware of both the appeal and the risks of supporting the exciting vision of these mission-centered entrepreneurs. However, your Crusader charisma and vision to make the world and markets better by tackling big problems can lure some investors who aren't prepared for the patience it will take to accomplish a mission of this magnitude.

Your Builder Personality has a gift for attracting early customers and followers. But many first-time Crusader entrepreneurs have not yet faced the practical difficulties and operational challenges to convert a big vision to lasting value in an indifferent, skeptical, or even hostile market environment. If that's you, beware of joining forces with a venture firm or early-stage investors that have not supported your kind of builder before.

First-time Crusaders need a capital partner willing to apply a heavy hand on the tiller at certain key moments in the development of their company. Your charismatic nature can inadvertently make this expert supervision a bit tricky. Take Nate Morris, for instance. His company, Rubicon Global, aspires to be the Uber of garbage. The exciting ambition of Morris's vision, combined with his impressive early customers such as Wegmans, Walmart, and The Home Depot, have allowed him to attract many famous sponsors, including John Ashcroft (former attorney general) and Leonardo DiCaprio. However, it was an experienced investor, Peter Kellner at Richmond Global, who pushed Morris to hire the right operational team and tighten the focus on profitability and efficiencies of scale.

The challenge for some Crusaders is they can attract investors without the necessary expertise or capital structure—investors drawn in more by the builder's vision than worried about the operational reality of how the company can convert idea to value. A string of impressive customer wins or favorable press can confound this challenge, postponing the day of financial reckoning. However, most investors— public or private—will eventually expect the business to generate positive earnings. At that point, rhetoric, however inspiring, will not trump actual results in the market: number of customers, revenue trajectory, cash flow, capital efficiency, and the like.

This gap between mission and financial reality can be particularly difficult if you're a Crusader working inside an established corporation. Here, it may be easier for potential sponsors to spot you than to support you. Sometimes, the crusades you advocate may be seen as competing with the current mission of the company or are maybe just confusing to the internal workforce or outside customers. So as we suggested above, before you ask for funding from an inside sponsor, you should carefully assess how well your crusade aligns with the strategy, brand, heritage, and culture of your company.

If your Crusader vision is compatible with, or complementary to, where your organization is headed, unleashing your prodigious builder skills can be a game changer. Perhaps your company needs a fresh infusion of passion and purpose to galvanize its troops or reposition itself in the minds of its market. In these cases, you may be just the right catalyst to advance your firm's growth agenda. In fact, your firm may have some things to learn itself from the leadership style and skills you bring to bear in inspiring followers to embark on that quest.

Furthermore, as with your Explorer counterparts, your corporate sponsor may be able to surround you with the very kind of operational get-it-done skills that prevail in most companies. As we've seen with builders like Nate Morris and Angelo Pizzagalli, Crusaders tend to focus on longer-range objectives and are comfortable with delegating large swaths of the routine operations to others. Making it easier and faster for you to recruit a fully functioning team can turbocharge your Builder Personality.

Your insider sponsor will have to strike a fine balance here between a legitimate concern about operational execution under your leadership as a Crusader and your need to build your form of new business value with your own distinctive personality. Too much over-the-shoulder monitoring on the sponsor's part may stifle the very spirit your Crusader style can foster in your team.

If the mission you can get chartered is strategic enough, chances are it—and you—will generate ripple effects in the existing organization. Other executives may question the urgency of this new agenda and be reluctant to give or share important resources under their control. Watch out for the kind of tokenism this attitude can produce. For example, an executive might free up a mediocre staffer to appear to support your mission. You and your sponsor need to keep translating the importance of your expedition to the people running today's operation.

Crusades are not for the faint of heart or the light of wallet. But they can be amazingly fruitful endeavors worth patience and investment commensurate with your own distinctive vision and leadership prowess. As an independent Crusader, try to recruit compatible investors that not only share your passion for the goal but also can shore up some of your limitations as you scale the business. And if you're a corporate Crusader looking for internal investment support, strive to match the promise of your mission with the premise of your company's own strategic vision and cultural roots.

Whether you are working outside or inside an existing company, as a Crusader you are likely to need investors comfortable with the somewhat longer, and probably more expensive, runway your business will need to lift off. The more explicitly you can align your respective expectations and agree on interim progress milestones, the better—for both of you. Switching metaphors, you can ill afford to have sponsors looking for the first off ramp on what will probably be a long road ahead.

Endowing the Captain:
Securing Investors Who Value Teamwork and Track Record

If you're a Captain, you build for growth in a manner attractive to many sponsors, particularly those who tend to back proven team leaders rather than untested entrepreneurs, hot product ideas, or trendy markets. They gain comfort in the way you build, whether you do so in an independent venture or a corporate one. You attract and inspire talented teams that are loyal to you and focused on your clearly articulated vision for the business. You are pragmatic, and you carefully manage your investors' expectations for how you will methodically prosecute your plan. You manage under the mantra "no surprises," carefully delivering on your commitments and perhaps even underpromising and overdelivering, both practices that build trust and confidence with many investors.

In startups, more conservative financial sponsors are most likely the best fit for you. These investors would prefer you grow more slowly and conserve cash, rather than risk a higher burn rate in hopes of winning the race to an installed user base or a land-grab strategy. It's important you find backers who share your steady-as-she-goes method of piloting your ship.

In fact, investors who like to back Captains may want to build a stable of them, supporting them from venture to venture. These Captains are seasoned leaders who can be good stewards of invested capital, and many can claim to deliver consistently strong returns. We have seen venture firms like Highland Capital Partners and Venrock execute such a strategy over decades.

Sponsors with more of a "swing for the fence" expectation may not be a good fit, because they're likely to be frustrated by your more conservative, methodical approach. Some Silicon Valley investors push Captain CEOs to pursue growth more aggressively than the executives are comfortable with. In these cases, the multiple bets embedded in the sponsor's portfolio may encourage them to be more risk prone than the builder, whose entire net worth is often tied up in his or her company.

We encourage you, if you're a Captain, to spend extra time with your prospective sponsors confirming alignment on growth rate, risk, and exit expectations. Ironically, your own track record of successful leadership may attract sponsors that are not an ideal fit, so beware.

Corporate Captains are often the favored sons and daughters of executive management for many of the same reasons their startup counterparts find it easier to attract sponsors. If you're such a Captain, your collaborative style and mindset tend to be highly valued in large, complex companies. Unlike builders in the independent startup world, corporate Captains may be tapped by senior executives to lead a new initiative that was not the Captain's idea to begin with, rather than seeking support for a venture of their own choosing.

Large companies—not to mention consulting and accounting firms, investment banks, or commercial lenders—are target-rich environments. They can present many value-creating possibilities that may be the perfect assignment for a Captain. If you work for such a firm, your executive team may have already identified a promising opportunity for significant value creation either within or outside the firm's current business portfolio. For example, a new product or line of business, an acquisition of another company with intriguing technology, or even a new business model that needs testing. In any event, the opportunity needs a leader. Frequently, a corporate Captain-in-the-making gets named to take on such an initiative, simply because the person has that glimmer of an entrepreneurial spirit.

The issue here is not that one Builder Personality is better than another (they're not). But it may be easier for a Captain operating inside a corporation to mesh with established cultural expectations and processes to get a new value initiative off the ground and onto a growth trajectory. However, as a corporate Captain, you will still need executive sponsorship to run occasional interference when you encounter obstacles working through normal channels and procedures.

As a Captain operating inside an established corporation, you have another key resource to fuel your growth: talent. You should try to secure your share of the best draft picks from within your company's ranks, while also retaining the freedom to go outside as necessary. Don't jump to the conclusion your best team members are other insiders. After time spent in corporate-style positions, insiders may well lack the instinct, style, and truly entrepreneurial spirit that's required. Because a good Captain will assess what skill sets he or she needs, be ready to ask your sponsors for whatever exceptions to your normal HR policies your outside-talent acquisition may necessitate.

As a corporate Captain, you can tap a host of other resources, including market and technology monitoring, to fuel your venture's growth. If you have particularly astute research and strategic thinkers in your company, involve them—as advisers and other resources—with your efforts. This kind of knowledge transfer seldom comes with the bureaucratic baggage of the other resources under your control and can keep your peripheral vision tuned to important trends in the marketplace.

Similarly, you can leverage your Captain's operational strengths by accessing appropriate systems, channels, and parties active in your current business. For example, you might expedite connections with distribution systems, access existing customer relationships, and piggyback onto your company's purchasing networks. These kinds of resource linkages can add real muscle in growing your venture, provided the overhead burden and procedural complexity involved don't out-weigh those potential efficiency and scale benefits.

However they may come to their roles, Captains are also likely to be much less fiery as corporate entrepreneurs than their other three counterparts. After all, Captains are consensus builders and problem solvers with a keen focus on operational execution—instincts not far removed from their fellow corporate colleagues. Drivers may have long since lost patience with the sclerotic decision making and risk aversion that often characterize incumbent businesses. They have either left or may be working in frustrated isolation. Explorers may struggle with building an interdisciplinary crew whose style and processes mesh with the host culture. And Crusaders may provoke a disruptive tug-of-war that competes, or even conflicts, with the company's existing mission and vision.

As either a startup or corporate Captain, you may have a some-what easier time securing the investor sponsors you're looking for than your other three builder counterparts. You tend to be no-drama Builders, willing to keep strategy and team closely aligned. Your abil-ity to build and manage teams that get things done is an attractive strength in both independent and corporate venture settings. Espe-cially for startup Captains seeking investors, you should not be shy about stressing the capabilities of the individuals you've assembled, and you should let potential investors take their measure directly with-out the kind of center-stage needs your three counterparts sometimes fall prey to.

Despite these advantages Captains enjoy, your longer-term chal-lenge with financial sponsors may arise precisely because of your strength as a team Captain. Sometimes, customers and markets are ripe for truly breakthrough, even breathtaking, disruption of the sort that Drivers, Explorers, and Crusaders propose, spikiness and all. But Captains tend not to get behind these kinds of radical opportunities.

So stand ready to periodically challenge your own Captain defaults to creatively and boldly evaluate where the real gold is in the mountains you are prospecting.

If you're an independent builder, understanding how your personality best matches with various styles and preferences of investors can help narrow your search for funding. And if your business is an acquisition candidate by a larger company, you need to anticipate how well you and the culture you have imprinted will mesh with the potential acquirer. This step is critically important, at least if you're interested in more than a take-the-money-and-run outcome or have an earn-out tied to the postacquisition performance of your company.

Similarly, if you are an employee eager to become a corporate business builder or if you join such an initiative, you also need to pay attention to how you can best align your aspiration with the underlying strategic agenda of your company. Most firms are short on the kind of gutsy champion talent you have to offer, but you have to be an adroit player of the inside game to get the resources you need to launch and grow your idea. And be creative in thinking about the range of non-financial internal resources you might need to tap in nurturing your business concept, perhaps even while developing it under the radar of your company's usual business procedures.

And finally, if you happen to be an investor in a startup, an acquirer of an ongoing business, or a sponsor of a venture, you will improve your own odds for success by understanding the personalities of the builders at the center of those businesses. Finding, matching, and supporting them may well be your best shot at growing your own business, as well as helping them grow theirs.

PART THREE

BECOMING THE BEST BUILDER YOU CAN BE

Strategies for Enhancing Your Impact

We close our book with a builder improvement section. First, on the next pages, you will see a summary set of profiles of each Builder Type along with their respective gifts and gaps for comparison. Then, in chapter 9, we offer two strategies to enhance your own craft as a builder.

The expert builder strategy is based on the elevate-and-delegate insights we shared in each Builder Personality chapter (chapters 2 through 5). It suggests you focus on honing your notable gifts, and delegate other important tasks to others. It's like a naturally gifted butterfly swimmer concentrating on that event, improving his or her stroke mechanics, rather than trying to develop flip turns for the breaststroke.

The master builder strategy, on the other hand, invites you to explore what lies beneath and beyond your natural strengths and style preferences, and examine why you do what you do. This takes real courage but, in turn, can allow you to borrow some of the techniques and approaches from what we call your polar complement. This is the Builder Type whose core strength may be your greatest deficit. With this strategy, you don't *become* someone else, but rather adopt and adapt your complement's strengths in a manner that makes them your own.

Whichever growth strategy you choose—expert or master—depends on your willingness to expose yourself . . . to yourself. Entrepreneurship is itself an exercise in personal exposure—to the public, the market, and one's colleagues, family, and friends. As a builder, you know how that feels. Regardless of your strategy, you will be on your way to becoming a stronger builder.

Builder Personality Type Snapshots: Factors

	Motivation	Decision-Making Mode
DRIVER	Always seen himself or herself as an entrepreneur. Ignited by ideas, driven to commercialize them with a fervor that feeds his or her self-confidence.	Initially intuition-based, but then seeks data and other external points of reference to triangulate and refine decisions.
EXPLORER	Sees entrepreneurship as a systematic way to commercialize and scale solutions to the knotty problems that he or she is most curious about.	Believes every problem should be systematically broken down into its constituent parts and carefully analyzed in order to make the best decision.
CRUSADER	Solving problems that matter to society, markets, or both. Rooted in empathy with others. Motivated to create a mission-based company.	Highly intuitive and driven from an emotional sense of what is right. Insists on alignment with overarching mission.
CAPTAIN	To build an enterprise of enduring value through unleashing the productive potential of individuals and teams.	Dispassionate and focused on growth. Careful to be consistent with mission, vision.

Management Approach	Leadership Style
Hands-on, directive, exacting with low or no tolerance for failure.	Results- and outcomes-focused, tends to attract and inspire like-minded perfectionists. Has a harder time with followers who are not equally driven and goal-oriented.
Hands-on, directive, and expects everyone to be as systematic and curious as he or she is.	Tends to attract similar systems thinkers; builds confidence in others after they've demonstrated systematic problem solving and deep knowledge.
Guided by their founding mission and intuition. Struggles with tough people issues, as he or she eschews conflict and often allows underperformers to languish rather than be ushered out.	Attracts followers to handle the more operational aspects of the business, inspiring them with vision and company mission, but not always directing them in a systematic manner.
Direct, honest, and consistent in communication and expectations of individuals and teams.	Empowers others after setting clear goals and expectations, while consistently applying deeply held principles of honesty and transparency. Consensus-driven.

Builder Personality Type Snapshots:
Gifts and Gaps

	Gifts (Strengths)	Gaps (Weaknesses)
DRIVER	• Uses combination of intuition and fact-based analysis to anticipate market trends before competitors. • Tenacity, ambition, and clear focus minimize distractions.	• Overidentification with product can miss new market shifts. • Impatience with customers who don't see your product's appeal. • May struggle with empowering team as company scales.
EXPLORER	• Systems thinking and analytics. • Focused on constant improvement and solving the next problem. • Scaling on the systems side can be easier.	• Scaling on the people side may be problematic, especially in functions outside your interest. • Brusque, impatient style can create morale problems. • Can get sucked into solving less strategic problems.
CRUSADER	• Inspires with bold vision conveyed with charisma. • Willing to delegate to others. • Comfortable with more flexible, creative workplace environment. • Has personal touch in dealing with others.	• Struggles with translating vision into practical to-dos. • Vulnerable to hiring on vision enthusiasm versus competency. • Conflict avoidance can let problems fester.
CAPTAIN	• Empowers others within regimen of clear accountability. • Encourages team member candor. • Willing to share credit for positive outcomes. • Open to "bubble-up" versus top-down creativity.	• Overdelegating can hide frontline developments. • May allow search for consensus to postpone fast decisions. • Focus on incremental improvements may miss need for innovation.

9

EXPANDING YOUR REPERTOIRE

Growing Beyond the Limits of Your Own Personality

One of the most remarkable aspects of human beings is our ability to learn and adapt. The most successful business builders tend to be very good at this process. In this chapter, we suggest specific ways you can grow and adapt to enhance your craft as a builder.

You have an ability not only to understand how and why your personality operates as it does, but also to deliberately alter how you apply your gifts by broadening your repertoire of skills and approaches. In other words—regardless of where you are in the arc of your career, we encourage you to look at your personality as a work in progress, more like a moving picture than a snapshot. We believe you can directly affect the way your personality influences how you build your business from startup to scale-up.

John Crowley: Master Builder in Progress

When we met John Crowley in 2014, he was clearly a full-fledged Captain.[1] He knew how to empower and guide his employees, who ranged from scientists to sales and marketing professionals to patient care coordinators. His vision for the second company he founded, Amicus, is very clear: to use biotechnology to create new medicines to cure the ravages of rare diseases that conventional pharmaceutical companies had either passed by or been stumped by.

Our hunch, though, is that Crowley was born a Driver. His dad was a police officer in Bergen County, New Jersey, and his mother a schoolteacher. He was accepted to the US Naval Academy and then went on to Harvard Business School for his MBA. This former Navy SEAL adviser is used to command authority, giving orders in high-stress situations. As you will recall, it was when two of his young children were diagnosed with Pompe disease—a virtual death sentence—that those Driver instincts were activated to find a cure.

In those days, Crowley was hard-driving, impatient, and relentless; he had a sixth sense of the market and how to capitalize on it. However, as he matured as a builder, he found his inner Captain, realizing that to attract and manage scientists, investors, and others, he needed to develop broader, more empowering skills of leadership in addition to honing his innate commercial sense alone.

Crowley sums up his journey: "I used to think I knew it all and didn't need any help or advice. And now I realize just how much I didn't know. In fact, I am amazed I did anything right back then, knowing and being a bit more stubborn."

Two Strategies for Becoming a Better Builder:
Expert or Master

While there are many ways for builders to become more effective, we will focus on the two strategies we see emerging from our research. The first we call the *expert builder strategy*, which is the logical extension of the elevate-and-delegate recommendations we described in each personality chapter. Paul Maeder, the former chairman of the National Venture Capital Association, told us: "I don't really care which builder personality you are. Just be the best darned version of your type you can be!"[2] This strategy involves elevating and focusing on your particular expertise and then, within each growth dynamic, delegating to others the roles and tasks in which you may be less skilled or less inspired.

The second approach is the *master builder strategy*. This involves learning and adopting some of the skills and techniques of the other Builder Personalities, starting with the person who best handles the growth dynamic and scaling stage you find the most challenging. As described throughout the book, the foundational expertise of each Builder Personality is as follows:

- Drivers are expert at product–market fit. They can accurately sense an emerging market need (not only where it is, but where it is headed) and have a keen commercial sense that allows them to translate those insights into demonstrable value to customers.

- Explorers excel at solving complex and strategically significant customer problems. They understand the underlying systems at play, and their constant curiosity leads them to engineer better solutions to material economic problems and opportunities.

- Crusaders inspire teams with powerful missions based on aligning mutual interests to achieve a better outcome. They attract truly engaged and dedicated followers by offering a worthy sense of purpose and pride among their employees and customers.

- Captains build durable cultures with strong executional focus. Their preference for collaboration breeds mutual accountability, openness, and an ability to deliver consistent financial results.

Your path to becoming a master builder requires expanding your management and leadership skills, much as a champion athlete does when developing and then mastering an entirely new shot, stroke, or kick. You don't become another personality; you just borrow and adapt a selection of their best features and make them your own.

So how does each builder type get to the point in his or her personal and professional development to have the motivation—even inspiration and courage—to begin pursuing the master builder strategy?

The paths to mastery—whether they lead through triumph or tragedy, intention or serendipity—are unpredictable. Regardless of path, the builder ready to pursue the master builder strategy recognizes that something more needs to change to enable him or her to reach the next level of effectiveness and even fulfillment. Of course we each bring our own unique set of scars reflecting agonizing failures, along with the trophies that memorialize our successes. In fact, it may be the combination of these two extremes that leads to the willingness to consider the master builder strategy. These extremes of experience and the learning that comes out of them can spark both a wish and a capacity to go deeper and seek not just expertise but true mastery in one's approach.

How does a Driver gain the wisdom that he should look to the natural leadership strengths of the Captain? Perhaps it comes from finally reaching the success he or she drove so hard to achieve and then having to courageously confront the alienation of others that was its cost. How about Explorers? What set of experiences catalyzes the realization that the empathic relationship building of the Crusader can draw and keep followers more deeply than the intellectual magnetism of the next gnarly problem? Perhaps—like the Driver—the very success and emptiness that can follow leads this systems thinker to realize the human system of emotional connection is both more complex and powerful than the safer domains to which he or she has tended to retreat.

Why do many Crusaders find so much satisfaction in the big idea, but lack the patience to work it through? Maybe for some it takes failure or being beaten by a competitor who had the same lofty mission, but also the discipline to out-execute him or her. From the wounds of that kind of disappointment can come the motivation to see the virtue in the Explorer's disciplined systematic thinking.

And finally, how about the Captain, who can be so gifted in tapping the collaborative productivity of others through delegation and empowerment, but may be reluctant to really step into the spotlight of personal accountability? Perhaps that is not an indication of humility but self-doubt and fear, in which case the Driver's defiant chip-on-the-shoulder gutsiness might be instructive to avoid getting blindsided by a tectonic shift in the market.

Regardless of how you get to this inflection point, you might consider the companionship and objectivity of an executive coach in helping pursue this master builder trajectory. And speaking as one who has (Chris here) partnered with a wonderful coach, he or she can make such a threatening path far less so and perhaps even enjoyable.

As you saw in each Builder Personality (chapters 2 through 5) and in figure 7-1, each type has advantages and disadvantages (gifts and gaps) across the five growth dynamics. Throughout this book, we have highlighted how one builder's gifts can be another's gaps, and vice versa. We have called this the *polar complement* phenomenon, where one personality's strength can be the model for addressing the other's weakness.

FIGURE 9-1

Whom Do You Think You Can Learn the Most From, and Where?

Now that you've read about all four Builder Personalities and how they handle each growth dynamic, we suggest you reflect on yourself. Think about the challenges and possibilities you've encountered or expect to encounter in each growth dynamic. Considering all five dynamics, decide which one plays most to your strengths, which one plays second-most, all the way down to which growth dynamic is your weakest. Mark a 1 in the square for your strongest growth dynamic, a 2 for your next-strongest, and so on. A 5 goes into your weakest dynamic. For the dynamics that scored 3 through 5, ask yourself which other Builder Personality probably does a better job than you in those dynamics. Your answer should give you a good sense of not just where you might want to focus your efforts, but also from whom you might best learn.

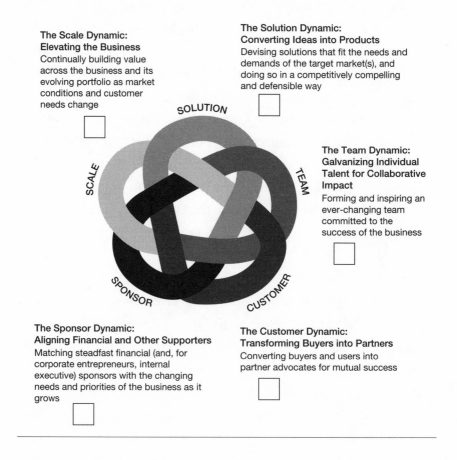

The Scale Dynamic: Elevating the Business
Continually building value across the business and its evolving portfolio as market conditions and customer needs change

The Solution Dynamic: Converting Ideas into Products
Devising solutions that fit the needs and demands of the target market(s), and doing so in a competitively compelling and defensible way

The Team Dynamic: Galvanizing Individual Talent for Collaborative Impact
Forming and inspiring an ever-changing team committed to the success of the business

The Sponsor Dynamic: Aligning Financial and Other Supporters
Matching steadfast financial (and, for corporate entrepreneurs, internal executive) sponsors with the changing needs and priorities of the business as it grows

The Customer Dynamic: Transforming Buyers into Partners
Converting buyers and users into partner advocates for mutual success

Specifically, we see the Driver and Captain as polar complements, as are the Explorer and Crusader. We will examine these pairs in more detail in each master builder section below.

As you consider which strategy might work best for you, figure 9-1 presents a simple exercise that may help you decide from which Builder Personality you could learn the most, and in what growth dynamics.

Recognizing that each builder can vary a bit within his or her Builder Personality Type's characteristics, we offer our suggestions of which types may have particular strengths worth considering in each growth dynamic:

Dynamic	Builder Personality Strengths
• Solution	Drivers and Explorers
• Team	Captains and Crusaders
• Customer	Drivers and Crusaders
• Sponsor	All four, each in its own way
• Scale	Captains and Explorers

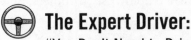

The Expert Driver:
"You Don't Need to Drive Everything"

Some Drivers may decide to focus within the comfort of their own sandbox and hire a CEO to lead and manage their organizations. As you saw in chapter 6, we urge builders to separate the math of equity ownership from the roles and responsibilities of managing the business. Drivers who elect the expert builder strategy continue doing what they are most innately talented in and love the most, building and continuously evolving the product to capitalize on their view of the ever-changing market. These Drivers may delegate responsibility by handing the CEO keys to a professional manager and retaining the role of chief product officer or perhaps nonexecutive chairman of the board.

In this strategy, you do not attempt to change your underlying Driver personality. You will remain a demanding person to work for. But this approach frees you to do what you do best—convert your market-sensing gift to identify your company's next round of products and services, while delegating the aspects of scale, such as building a collaborative culture, that are better led by others who naturally have these gifts.

The Driver as Master Builder:
"Release the Wheel, Empower like a Captain"

The monolithic product and market focus of the Driver can crowd out the development of this personality's broader leadership skills, which are the Captain's gifts. Let's take a more careful look at how this plays out across the stages of scaling the business.

In the startup of your business, if you're a Driver, your laser-like focus and gift of sensing market direction enabled you to fit your initial product to the market and win over early employees, customers, and investors. Now, over the first few stages of growth, your energy and tenacity can continue to be the propulsion. However, as the business grows to hundreds of employees who are working across geographically disparate offices, not even Drivers have the power and reach to direct and motivate the way they did in the early days.

At these latter stages of scale and beyond, all builders need motivated, capable building crews. The assembling of such crews is the particular gift of the Captain. So, as a Driver, if you aspire to the master builder strategy, you should look to borrow from the strengths and techniques of the Captain, your polar complement. A Captain approaches building through others in a deliberate manner and sows the seeds early, well before they must be reaped. This builder sees his or her primary role as attracting and cultivating talent. A Captain does this with a careful eye on the skills needed for both today's and tomorrow's levels of scale.

Drivers should learn early to begin overhiring for each role by selecting people who may be somewhat overqualified today but are well prepared to handle scaling. Overhiring for key roles has the benefit of correcting another Driver tendency. Drivers' natural inclination is to hold on to the wheel, as opposed to training and teaching others to handle it. When you overhire for a key role, more-experienced people will probably require you to back off or they will not accept or stay in the position.

The other technique you can borrow from Captains is their ability to build scalable, empowered teams with very clear roles, responsibility, and accountability. This clarity can temper your overcontrolling instincts. If you can let go of the specifics but retain clear accountability for results, you may achieve the desired outcome without having to do it all yourself. Focus on what your team members get done, not so much on how they do it.

You may well find that by broadening your objective from market success at all costs to *team* success, you can achieve the former through succeeding with the latter. This perspective comes easily to the Captain, but requires Drivers to choose between their ambition for impact and their need for control. The very thing that allowed the Driver to achieve one level of success now holds him or her back.

Adam Jackson, the cofounder of Doctor On Demand introduced earlier in the book, came to terms with this tension in early 2016, when he handed the leadership reins of his company to a more experienced builder who had recently been a senior leader at PayPal. Jackson told us, "I reconcile things in order of the goals. The goal for me is to build the biggest and most successful behemoth in our space. So I must recruit those who are better than me, empower them, communicate the vision clearly, and let go." Drivers who attain the skills of a master builder combine their native product-and market-sensing gifts with the leadership skills of the Captain.

 ## The Expert Explorer:
"Concentrate on Your Passion and Gift for Problem Solving"

As an Explorer, you may feel your highest contribution to ongoing value creation is not in the role of CEO. Regardless of the actual titles you may choose, your de facto role might be better as the company's chief product officer or chief innovation officer. These functions play to your underlying and likely enduring strengths and interests. That said, Explorer teams should consider nontraditional organizational and reporting structures that offer your kind of builders some sandbox possibilities for your curiosity to roam free of the bureaucracy.

Brian O'Kelley is an Explorer who selected the expert builder strategy. He has remained in his sandbox by "going ninja"—that is, instead of trying to influence a large project team from behind the doors of his C-suite, he works directly with a few product engineers. This unconventional approach is his explicit signal to the organization that he is focusing on his gift of problem solving. The approach runs contrary to the conventional role of a CEO, who would take care not to disrupt the chain of command.

In this approach, O'Kelley *is* the product manager and works directly with that small team of engineers to solve the next gnarly growth problem—this in a company with well over a thousand employees and an enterprise some guess to be worth more than $2 billion. So who provides the human touch of reaching and motivating the troops day in and day out? Well, O'Kelley has created a troika that actually manages the business: Michael Rubenstein as president, Jonathan Hsu, as COO, and O'Kelley. In the case of AppNexus, it looks like the elevate-and-delegate strategy is working pretty well.

The Explorer as Master Builder:
"Adopt the Human Touch of the Crusader"

If you are an Explorer, your systems thinking serves you well across the more mechanical aspects of the business, such as translating ideas into products, engaging sophisticated customers and investors, and planning for scaling the business. However, you may not be tapping your followers' human need for purpose and mission beyond the problem-solving core on which you have built the business.

Explorers derive confidence and control over the world around them by studying and then developing an integrated understanding of the mechanism or system at play. As you become better at solving the mechanics of problems, your confidence builds. With that can come a bit of a superiority complex that may drive a wedge between you and the team scaling the business. An executive coach or psychologist might call this depersonalizing the relationship. We call it taking the humanity out.

The key to scaling an already-successful business is to raise the level of commitment to the purpose of the enterprise above mere role and responsibility. Explorers who can create this higher-order purpose for the work end up recruiting and inspiring an entirely different level of workforce and, with it, increase their ability to scale.

As an Explorer, you should learn how to reach your followers on a more emotional rather than just a purely intellectual, commercial, or professional level. For this reason, the best teacher to help you become a master builder is the Crusader, your polar complement. Crusaders motivate and align others through an empathic connection with individuals across their organizations. Mark Bonfigli pursued this exact path as he saw the system at play in creating a high-energy culture with workout facility and costume parties to boot. As an Explorer, you have a set of preferences you can build on. You value honesty and transparency, which can be the building blocks of a deep and trusting relationship. These characteristics are necessary, but not sufficient.

An Explorer is often more concerned about being right, which he or she sees as a form of honesty, regardless of the emotional impact on coworkers. As an Explorer, you need to move beyond the safety of this form of honesty to one far scarier, one based on making *yourself* emotionally available and perhaps even vulnerable in your professional relationships.

Crusaders can teach you how to communicate and manage from a central mission and form an empathic connection to each member of your crew. It is that very mission that brought the Crusader into entrepreneurship in the first place. So we are not suggesting you become a missionary like the Crusader, but rather we are encouraging you to use mission as a managerial tool to reach and inspire others emotionally.

As mentioned earlier, Crusaders Ben Cohen and Jerry Greenfield provided their employees with such a sense of purpose that their workers would come in on weekends with their own tools to make sure the ice cream was being made correctly. Later, as the founders' business grew to several hundred million dollars in revenues, they imbued it with a sense of social mission, allowing employees to take time off from work to attend rallies in the famous branded Cowmobile (the brightly painted truck featuring cows in a Vermont field).

This socially aware mission with a Vermont folksy style might seem goofy to the engineering mind of an Explorer. But you should look below the surface to discover the underlying mechanism at play. Cohen and Greenfield figured out a way to ensure the company they were building provided a sense of meaning and greater purpose in the lives of their employees, by baking (or perhaps churning) that ethos into the company. The committed employees then recruited like-minded folks to help scale the business.

In summary, if your hard-edged systems thinking as an Explorer softened to include the motivating mission of the Crusader, you might be unstoppable!

The Expert Crusader:
"Focus on Being the Standard-Bearer for the Mission, and Hire an Operator"

As a Crusader, you are arguably the strongest of our four builders when it comes to convincing others to make big things happen in a market or even the world. Frequently charismatic and articulate, you have a passion that can be infectious. You literally are a *game framer*, in that you can help others imagine an entirely different way of creating value—whether it's Rent the Runway, which makes the luxury of a fashion designer's dress affordable; Rubicon Global, which changes the economics of recycled garbage; or Ben & Jerry's, which connects eating ice cream with social change. In the expert builder strategy, you focus entirely on applying your gift of seeing, creating, and articulating the mission to customers, employees, and suppliers. You are the chief evangelist. Not only do you carry the flag of your company, but in many ways, you *are* the flag.

However, as a Crusader, your approach has two challenges. First, you tend to fly too high. Your focus on mission can cause you to pay too little attention to the operational aspects of the business. This problem can be confounded by the very strength we just said

Explorers should borrow from you—your clear compassion and human connection to your employees. In your case, this wonderful quality can result in an inability to glean underperformers and a reluctance to address conflict head-on. In short, your compassion can get the better of you.

If you adopt the expert builder strategy, you need to delegate the day-to-day aspects of your business to committed and trusted deputies who will build out and manage the details necessary to realize your mission. To delegate successfully, you need the right kind of operational leader, whose skills and style are quite different from yours. Since the selection and vetting of deep operational skills is not a natural strength of Crusaders by definition, it is important to select the right adviser to help. Outside investors, particularly those who specialize in your type of business or have an operating partner with functional expertise, can be a useful resource to close such an experience gap.

The Crusader as Master Builder:
"Borrow the Explorer's Systematic Approach"

Crusaders generate tremendous momentum from their mission and the charismatic way in which they get their employees, customers, and investors to follow them. As we have just said, Crusaders often lack a strong ability to operationalize the business at each level of scale—a natural strength of the Explorer.

So how can you become a master builder? Look to the systematic strengths of the Explorer, who can return the favor we suggested in the previous section.

You can learn much from your Explorer cousin—the master mechanic. But how might a compassionate and intuitive builder learn from one wired in the opposing manner? We believe the bridge to the Explorer's systems thinking lies in the Crusader's ability to sense and then capitalize on areas of misalignment. Both these builders are tapping into an understanding of the system at play.

The Explorer does this through a fact-based analysis, while the Crusader does so through an intuitive sense of needs and wants. If as a Crusader you can see operational issues through your sense of alignment, you may be on the path to adopting the Explorer's operational strengths, but you'll do so in your own way.

 **The Expert Captain:**
"Continue to Empower, Coach, and Listen"

If you're a Captain, your game centers on your team-centric leadership. This gift allows you to tap the inner drives of those who work for you, and then manage teams through vision, mutual accountability, and empowerment.

As a Captain, you excel at figuring out how to get the best out of both individuals and teams. In this strategy, you continue applying your finely honed skills of listening, delegating, and empowering your direct reports and their respective teams.

Expert Captains expand their leadership and management fluency. You probably are leading a more diverse group of team members than you were earlier in your career. To take further advantage of your leadership gift, spend more time familiarizing yourself with the crew's different ways of thinking, talking, and even listening. It's your chance to improve your ability to translate what needs to get done in your business into terms people can relate to . . . dude.

The delegation strategy for a Captain may sound counterintuitive. It requires you to go beyond active orchestration to actually handing over the baton to others to see if your band can play without you. If they can, this will expand your ability to reach and motivate the changing mix of players on your various teams.

The Captain as Master Builder:
"Test-Drive How the Driver Masters Market Changes and Product Fit"

Captains, as we have noted, are often the most well-rounded builders of our four. If you are a Captain, your innate strength is in selecting, assigning, and encouraging others to work collaboratively and tenaciously toward the common vision of the company. You are honest and transparent and thereby create a deep sense of trust across your employee base. You build and manage through others, holding each person accountable for clearly defined results.

So on what basis and from which fellow builder can you best learn if you want to pursue your own master builder strategy? We believe the Driver is your polar complement as a Captain. As we identified earlier, the Driver has much to learn from the Captain, but the inverse is also true, particularly as the company enters more competitive and faster-moving market conditions, which tend to accelerate with scale. As a Captain, you can enhance your effectiveness over time by taking on the problem- or solution-centered strengths of the Driver and Explorer, but without the overbearing ego of either of those Builder Types.

Recall that the Captains we have met tend to launch their businesses with a simple and pragmatic insight. Think of Suri Suriyakumar, who began to roll up small blueprinting operations, creating paper-purchasing efficiencies and geographic coverage to serve national construction firms. By late 2016, he was beginning to offer his clients cloud storage and retrieval capabilities for the blueprints his company created to inform a building's maintenance and, ultimately, its demolition over its full life cycle.

Under the master builder strategy, the Driver can provide you with a role model on how to ensure market shifts do not end up surprising you, leaving your pragmatic business out of touch with customers' underlying needs and wants. Recall how conscientiously Mi Jong Lee observed the underlying needs of her fashion customers. She was so in touch with their evolving needs that she was able to adapt with them, as opposed to being passed by in the fast-moving world of fashion.

To become better at discerning the market's changing path, you need to face one important challenge. You have to be willing to pull the team, and perhaps even yourself, out of its comfort zone. The bridge to operating against your preference for empowerment lies in your ambition. In fast-moving markets you may need to use your ambition to help you operate against your natural inclination and sacrifice a bit of team spirit to make a strategic pivot. Perhaps you can succeed by getting to the answer first, as Suriyakumar did, and then guiding your team to the product or market insight you have already gleaned.

Having opened this chapter with John Crowley's trajectory on the master builder path, we'll close with another example of how a builder can expand her repertoire—using one style to buffer the downside of another.

As a builder, you have undoubtedly learned, adapted, and grown dramatically as you've launched and managed your business thus far. We know what a grind the building process can be. We hope the strategies of this chapter and insights from earlier chapters will reinforce your enthusiasm for the challenge and rewards of building for growth.

Laurie Spengler: Master Builder in Progress

As described in chapter 2, Laurie Spengler built and sold a European financial advisory firm called the Central European Advisory Group.[3] In many respects, Spengler is a classic Driver. As Czechoslovakia split into the Czech Republic and Slovakia in 1993, this young woman from New Jersey could intuitively sense the market opportunity.

Companies that were emerging from the desolation of the Soviet-style command economy toward a market-driven one needed advice and guidance on capital sourcing and restructuring. This market-sensing and gutsy woman launched her business in an industry—and business climate—dominated by men.

As described earlier, Spengler has all the dynamism, confidence, and tenacity of the Driver. But she has considerably more. She has emerged as a master builder, taking on the mission awareness of the Crusader and the advanced leadership skills of a Captain.

In many respects, Spengler's motivation was that of a Crusader: "I wanted to contribute to a world that is not bifurcated between commercial results and philanthropy," she says, "but rather to advance business models and enable people to see that the world can be a blend of the best of both."

Her inner Crusader is further enhanced with the empowering leadership ethos of the Captain. She was inspired by her father, who was a successful entrepreneur and taught her that "success is driven by a broader view of stakeholders that includes employees, and providing them with good jobs, benefits, and the ability to send their kids to college." So when Spengler was thinking about selling her firm, she considered going for the capital-maximizing move and selling it to a big financial services company.

Instead, she decided to sell it to her own employees for less money. She explains her motivation as "seeding the next generation of entrepreneurs in the community where I had worked." She reflects back on this period: "I think this is my own maturation. It's less about my personality and more about my values. In my professional life, the anchor is my values, combined with my view of what I want the world to look like."

Laurie Spengler is thus a potential model master builder, intentionally integrating the strengths of the Driver, Crusader, and Captain.

A Closing Note

If building for growth is the imperative for your business, personality matters. Who you are shapes how you build your business, your team, and your ability to win. We hope this book has made this challenging imperative more achievable. Now you can decode, understand, and find your path to becoming a stronger builder—whether you're a Driver, an Explorer, a Crusader, or a Captain.

We have shown cobuilders how to vet and then fuse deeper and more productive partnerships, while supporting both them and their crews in identifying and selecting crew members who best match their goals and styles. And finally, we have suggested ways in which builders, investors, and corporate sponsors should select one another to maximize alignment of goals, approach, and style.

The task of building businesses of enduring value from scratch is enormously challenging. There are so many factors at play—things we can see, like competitors' actions, to things we cannot, such as secret technology breakthroughs. Macroeconomic forces buffet, buoy, or destroy, and of course, sheer luck is always playing behind the scenes.

Amid all these forces, personality is the one resource you the builder can control. Your personality is never as perfect or as flawed as you, your biggest fans, or your harshest critics may believe. But it is a uniquely powerful resource you can understand and leverage for greater impact. We hope we have armed you with the tools, stories, and practical suggestions on how to do just that.

Regardless of your Builder Personality, your work of starting, growing, and scaling your business is a vital endeavor that creates opportunity and fuels prosperity. Our economy, our societies, and our world depend on the growth your success makes possible.

Simply put, we need you, your team, and your business to be *built for growth*.

Appendix A

OUR RESEARCH METHODOLOGY

How We Decoded the Secrets of Entrepreneurial Builders

Over the thirteen years during which Chris and his team founded, built, and scaled Rosetta, they conducted thousands of Personality-Based Clustering assignments for many Global 1000 companies around the world. In this work, the Rosetta team analyzed over one million respondents across billions of observations. It served market leaders in health care, such as Johnson & Johnson, Genentech, Pfizer, and Bristol-Meyers Squibb; financial services companies like Chase, Fidelity, Capital One, and Citibank; consumer technology firms such as Samsung, Microsoft, and Activision; nonprofits like NPR and the Special Olympics; and hundreds of other companies. These insights were then used to define and execute personalized marketing campaigns based in markets around the world.

And the approach works. The results were dramatic—with an average improvement in marketing effectiveness (incremental revenue per dollar of marketing spent) that ranged from 75 percent to 150 percent more effective, and more. Those campaigns proved far more effective in driving consumer purchases and thereby marketing return on investment.

Rosetta's Personality-Based Clustering technique works in marketing because the tool separates consumers for each industry into distinct groups according to their motivations and preferences. With this understanding and a set of typing tools to target each group, the product, the message, and the offering can be personalized to the buying hot buttons of each group.

The Builder Typology

Having proven that Rosetta's Personality-Based Clustering methodology could decipher the mysteries of who buys what brands and why in marketplaces around the world, we worked with Rosetta to adapt that analytical engine to address the threshold issue of who builds those businesses in the first place, why and how. We focused on answering three questions: Which factors form and define distinct Builder Personalities? Who are the resulting Builder Types in terms of how their preferences drive their building behaviors? Finally, when we applied the Builder Personality Discovery (BPD) quiz to individual builders and then interviewed them intensely on the details of how they built their businesses, did we hear stories and examples consistent with the preferences of each type?

The Four Factors That Create Our Builder Typology

The ten-question BPD quiz we used in our interviews for this book represents the distillation of results from a more extensive survey instrument sent to several larger groups of successful business founders. That original instrument, comprising over one hundred questions, was completed by more than 450 respondents within a panel of builder CEOs who had achieved at least $3 million in annual revenue and had been in business for at least three years.[1] We further supplemented this group with members of the Young Presidents' Organization, the Women Presidents' Organization, and other professional groups containing large numbers of founders who met our criteria.

By applying Rosetta's patented clustering algorithm to the respondent data described above, we were able to isolate the four factors and their ten underlying dimensions that categorize the builder population into four distinct types. The factors and dimensions are as follows:

Motivation and Self-Identity

- Does the person feel he or she was always destined to be a business builder, or did it occur more by happenstance?
- To what degree does the person ascribe his or her success to luck and market timing?
- Does the person prefer to focus on selling or delivering the product or service?

Decision-Making Mode

- Does the person tend to rely more on intuition or the facts?
- Does the person encourage experimentation?

Management Approach

- Does the person consider his or her management team key to the venture's success?
- Does the person tend to be hands-on or laissez-faire?
- Does the person consider tough decisions personal or just part of business?

Leadership Style

- Does the person inspire people through empathy and compassion?
- Does the person consider the company "my company" or "our company"?

These factors and dimensions are reflected in the ten-question BPD quiz (see chapter 1 sidebar "Which Builder Personality Is Most Similar to Yours?"), powered by our algorithm on the www.builtforgrowth.com website.

Limitations of the Builder Personality Discovery (BPD) Quiz

Our BPD instrument shares the same limitations as those of other psychometric instruments (the fancy term for questionnaires that compare you with others and place you in a descriptive group, known as a type). Let's look at these limitations.

Consistency

The BPD tool, like the Myers-Briggs Type Indicator, the Hogan Personality Inventory, and other assessments, depends on your accurate and honest responses to the questions. Because people's answers may vary, depending on their mood, a person's frame of mind can change the results. This variation in typing is a limitation inherent in all these instruments, including our BPD tool.

Accuracy

Like consistency, accuracy in any instrument based on self-reported data depends on your honest responses and is vulnerable to how you might be feeling when you complete the instrument. Therefore, we encourage you to take our BPD quiz several times over the course of a week to ten days, under different situations—especially if you feel your initial typing isn't quite accurate. Repeating the survey will help you determine if there is a dominant type that emerges.

Another idea to consider is to ask two or three confidants whose opinion you value how they think you would probably answer the ten questions. After they have done this for you, quietly consider how close your respective answers are to theirs. In this way, you can check the objectivity of your own assessment.

Hybrids: Builders Who Are Blends of More Than One Builder Type

Few of us fit neatly in any personality box; nor is personality necessarily fixed in concrete. Some of us are blends, and our Builder Personalities are no different. People are inherently adaptive, watching and taking on qualities of others they work with or were mentored by. Of course, this adaptive approach can be a highly effective way to hone and diversify your building repertoire. We refer to this kind of adaptive blending as nurture-driven (you picked it up from your environment). The other kind of blending we call nature-driven, that is, your blended personality is psychologically hardwired in you. Think of the current discussions on gender and the emergent hypothesis that perhaps we should think of it as a spectrum, rather than just two points, male and female.

To reflect this concept of the blended personality, we use your responses to create a measure of the likelihood that you are a combination of two types and, if so, which two and in what proportions. This blended insight is only available on our website, because of the underlying statistics we must run to compare your responses with the test population. While we cannot distinguish between nurture- and nature-driven blends, we can tell if you are most like one of our Builder Types or a blend of two. So if you're curious, please visit our site at www. builtforgrowth.com.

You may be wondering about the difference between hybrid Builder Personalities and our concept of master builders. Hybrids are composites of two or more Builder Types, in which their Builder Personality is wired in a manner that shares core elements of more than one type. This is quite different from a builder who starts out as a distinct personality type with the gifts and gaps of that type. But as that builder develops professionally, he or she begins to understand how his or her preferences and biases create gaps. It is with this deeper understanding of self that the master builder can study his or her polar complement and deliberately take on that type's preferences, but do so by authentically making them his or her own.

An Overview of Personality Testing, and Where Personality-Based Clustering Fits

Although all of us may want to believe we are absolutely unique, there is actually a finite amount of variation in personality. The Rosetta Personality-Based Clustering technique borrowed conceptually from the seminal work of Katharine Cook Briggs and her daughter, Isabel Briggs Myers.

In the early 1940s, Briggs and Myers developed a psychometric questionnaire known as the Myers-Briggs Type Indicator. This instrument was designed to measure psychological preferences in how people perceive the world and make decisions. The original work by Myers and Briggs was used to help women during World War II find the jobs that best fit their temperament. Since its creation, this instrument has been administered many millions of times.

The insights gained from that pioneering work have since spawned an entire industry of personality testing, and Rosetta's Personality-Based Clustering technique has a specific place in this landscape. Although there are many ways to characterize them, you can classify psychometric personality typing tools based on the scope and nature of the populations they address. Figure A-1 depicts this as a funnel. At

FIGURE A-1

Examples of Personality Typing Tools

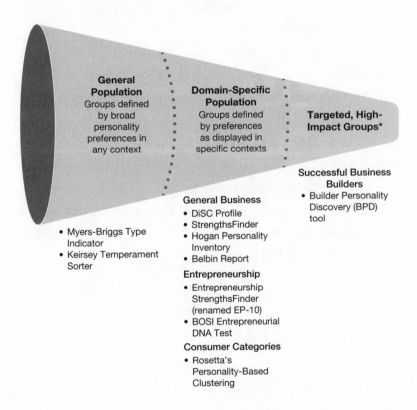

General Population
Groups defined by broad personality preferences in any context

- Myers-Briggs Type Indicator
- Keirsey Temperament Sorter

Domain-Specific Population
Groups defined by preferences as displayed in specific contexts

General Business
- DiSC Profile
- StrengthsFinder
- Hogan Personality Inventory
- Belbin Report

Entrepreneurship
- Entrepreneurship StrengthsFinder (renamed EP-10)
- BOSI Entrepreneurial DNA Test

Consumer Categories
- Rosetta's Personality-Based Clustering

Targeted, High-Impact Groups*

Successful Business Builders
- Builder Personality Discovery (BPD) tool

*These tools identify the specific beliefs, motivation, and preferences critical to success in the indicated context.

the wide end is general personality testing, a set of tools that can be applied to all people and explains significant variations in personality across the broad population. In the middle of the funnel are tools focused on more discrete, domain-specific populations, such as people who work in businesses or are considering entrepreneurship. The narrowest part of the funnel has even more highly specialized personality tools. Let's look at these three types of tools in more depth.

General Population Personality Tools

At the wide end of the funnel, the Myers-Briggs Type Indicator is the best-known example of this kind of broad tool. Based on the theories of Carl Jung, Briggs and Myers's work postulated that all potential human personalities could be profiled along four dimensions (introverted versus extroverted, sensing versus intuition, thinking versus feeling, and judgment versus perception), resulting in sixteen personality variations (the various combinations of four dimensions). For example, if you're an INTP, you tend to be more introverted (I), rely on your intuition (N), are more prone to thinking (T) than feeling, and approach life in an open-ended, perceiving (P) way, rather than judging (J). Figure A-2 describes the four dimensions and the spectrum of potential responses for the Myers-Briggs Type Indicator.

FIGURE A-2

The Four Dimensions of the Myers-Briggs Type Indicator

DIMENSION

1. Favorite World

External (outer world)	....	Source of energy	....	Internal (inner world)

2. Information

Facts (sensing)	....	Method of obtaining information	....	Possibilities (intuition)

3. Decisions

Head (thinking)	....	Approach to decision making	....	Heart (feeling)

4. Structure

Organized (judging)	....	Approach to life	....	Open-ended (perceiving)

Broad, Domain-Specific Personality Tools

In the middle of the funnel are broad, domain-specific psychometric tools. They are built on a construct similar to Myers-Briggs in that they identify factors that separate individuals within a specific domain, such as people in business or, even more specifically, those who might be interested in entrepreneurship.

In 1998, Chris and his team at Rosetta developed the idea of applying psychometric tools to specialized consumer populations. They created a process of building industry-specific tools to explain how and why individuals in various consumer categories ranging from credit cards and cell phones to pain relievers and clothing make purchase and brand choice decisions. Their initial hypothesis was that each of us, as consumers, brings a set of beliefs, motivations, and preferences that influence our category and brand-purchasing behavior.

For example, will I buy a new cell phone or not? If I will, what combination of beliefs (I think Apple makes better cell phones), motivations (the brand and style project what I want to my friends), and preferences (mix of voice and data functionality, price, service coverage, etc.) drive my cell phone purchasing behavior? Rosetta called this particular domain the Cell Phone Personality Typology and, over the years, used it to enhance the marketing effectiveness for AT&T Wireless, Sprint, and several well-known handset manufacturers. Rosetta built similar models to describe consumer choice across hundreds of categories around the world.

Another of these domain-specific tools is the StrengthsFinder tool from the Gallup Organization.[2] StrengthsFinder has been applied to hundreds of thousands of individuals to help them and their employers identify the test taker's innate strengths. With this information, employees can be placed in the most appropriate jobs and are sometimes helped along their professional-development path. In the last several years, Gallup adapted this tool to the question of who might be best suited to become an entrepreneur, as laid out in its *Entrepreneurial Strengths-Finder* book.[3] The book provides valuable insights to those trying to sort out whether they may have what it takes to become an entrepreneur.

Targeted, High-Impact Personality Tools

At the narrow end of the funnel is a set of highly specialized personality tools that are applied to unique populations to separate people into subgroups according to how their beliefs and preferences explicitly drive their choices and behaviors in very specific domains. The BPD tool we developed with Rosetta's methodology—and then applied to the high-impact group of successful entrepreneurs—is just such an instrument. It is specifically designed to discover the underlying personality profiles of the builders of successful new businesses.

It does so by creating a broad spectrum of potential responses, as shown in figure A-3, to the BPD tool. Most of the questions are measured on a seven-point scale, and the others with yes-or-no answers.

FIGURE A-3

The Four Factors and Underlying Dimensions of the Builder Personality Discovery (BPD) tool

FACTOR

1. Motivation and Self-Identity

Happenstance	Motivation to be a business builder	Destiny
Not important	Role of luck and timing in success	Important
Delivering product/service	Role preference	Selling product/ service

2. Decision-Making Mode

Fact-based	Approach	Intuition-based
Do not favor	Culture of experimentation	Favor

3. Management Approach

Less important	Role of management team	Critical to success
Laissez-faire	Need for control	Control freak
Personal	Consider tough decisions	Just part of business

4. Leadership Style

"Not key to my leadership"	Compassion and empathy	"Key to my leadership"
"Our company"	Think of the company as	"My company"

Appendix B

BUILDER ARCHETYPES

Response Patterns for Each Builder Type

As you compare your response pattern to the Builder Personality Quiz you took in chapter 1 to the patterns shown in the following section, please keep in mind some of points of context:

- There is a wide variety in response to these questions even within a Builder Personality. Here we are providing just the archetype patterns to give you a point of comparison for your pattern so you can see which one you tend to be most like. The archetype patterns also provide you with a higher-level view of how each of the four factors separates each type from the others.

- Do not be concerned if your pattern does not tightly match one of the archetypes shown here because the quiz in the book is a simplified version of the one you will find on our website, in which seven of the questions have a seven-point response scale, rather than the simplified three-point scale here. The more granular response scale measures your beliefs and preferences with greater resolution and thereby predicts your Builder Type with greater accuracy.

- The full-response-scale version of the quiz, available on our website (www.builtforgrowth.com), has more than one billion response combinations across these questions, which is why the most accurate way to discover your type is to go to the site and complete the quiz with the full scale.

🎯 Driver (archetype)

MOTIVATION & SELF-IDENTITY

1. I always knew I would start my own business one day.

   Disagree　　　　　**Neutral**　　　　　(**Agree**)

2. I consider luck, timing, and market conditions to be the most important reason for my success.

   (**No**)　　　　　**Yes**

3. I am more energized by selling versus delivering the product/service.

   (**Selling**)　　　　　**Neutral**　　　　　**Delivering**

DECISION-MAKING MODE

4. When framing a problem, I rely mostly on the facts versus I rely mostly on my intuition.

   Facts　　　　　**Neutral**　　　　　(**Intuition**)

5. Our company culture strongly encourages experimentation.

   Disagree　　　　　**Neutral**　　　　　(**Agree**)

MANAGEMENT APPROACH

6. I consider my management team/staff to be one of the most important reasons for my success.

   (**No**)　　　　　**Yes**

7. Most of my friends and colleagues would consider me a control freak.

   Disagree　　　　　(**Neutral**)　　　　　**Agree**

8. I don't consider tough business decisions personal. I just see them as part of business.

   Disagree　　　　　**Neutral**　　　　　(**Agree**)

LEADERSHIP STYLE

9. I inspire people to follow me primarily through my compassion/empathy.

   (**No**)　　　　　**Yes**

10. I consider the company as MY company versus OUR company.

    (**My company**)　　　　　**Neutral**　　　　　**Our company**

⚙ Explorer (archetype)

MOTIVATION & SELF-IDENTITY

1. I always knew I would start my own business one day.

   (Disagree)   Neutral   Agree

2. I consider luck, timing, and market conditions to be the most important reason for my success.

   (No)   Yes

3. I am more energized by selling versus delivering the product/service.

   Selling   Neutral   (Delivering)

DECISION-MAKING MODE

4. When framing a problem, I rely mostly on the facts versus I rely mostly on my intuition.

   (Facts)   Neutral   Intuition

5. Our company culture strongly encourages experimentation.

   (Disagree)   Neutral   Agree

MANAGEMENT APPROACH

6. I consider my management team/staff to be one of the most important reasons for my success.

   (No)   Yes

7. Most of my friends and colleagues would consider me a control freak.

   Disagree   Neutral   (Agree)

8. I don't consider tough business decisions personal. I just see them as part of business.

   Disagree   Neutral   (Agree)

LEADERSHIP STYLE

9. I inspire people to follow me primarily through my compassion/empathy.

   (No)   Yes

10. I consider the company as MY company versus OUR company.

    My company   (Neutral)   Our company

🏴 Crusader (archetype)

MOTIVATION & SELF-IDENTITY

1. I always knew I would start my own business one day.
   (Disagree)   Neutral   Agree

2. I consider luck, timing, and market conditions to be the most important reason for my success.
                    No   (Yes)

3. I am more energized by selling versus delivering the product/service.
   Selling   (Neutral)   Delivering

DECISION-MAKING MODE

4. When framing a problem, I rely mostly on the facts versus I rely mostly on my intuition.
   Facts   (Neutral)   Intuition

5. Our company culture strongly encourages experimentation.
   Disagree   (Neutral)   Agree

MANAGEMENT APPROACH

6. I consider my management team/staff to be one of the most important reasons for my success.
                    No   (Yes)

7. Most of my friends and colleagues would consider me a control freak.
   Disagree   (Neutral)   Agree

8. I don't consider tough business decisions personal. I just see them as part of business.
   (Disagree)   Neutral   Agree

LEADERSHIP STYLE

9. I inspire people to follow me primarily through my compassion/empathy.
                    No   (Yes)

10. I consider the company as MY company versus OUR company.
    My company   (Neutral)   Our company

247

👥 Captain (archetype)

MOTIVATION & SELF-IDENTITY

1. I always knew I would start my own business one day.
   (Disagree)   Neutral   Agree

2. I consider luck, timing, and market conditions to be the most important reason for my success.
   (No)   Yes

3. I am more energized by selling versus delivering the product/service.
   Selling   Neutral   **(Delivering)**

DECISION-MAKING MODE

4. When framing a problem, I rely mostly on the facts versus I rely mostly on my intuition.
   (Facts)   Neutral   Intuition

5. Our company culture strongly encourages experimentation.
   Disagree   Neutral   **(Agree)**

MANAGEMENT APPROACH

6. I consider my management team/staff to be one of the most important reasons for my success.
   No   **(Yes)**

7. Most of my friends and colleagues would consider me a control freak.
   (Disagree)   Neutral   Agree

8. I don't consider tough business decisions personal. I just see them as part of business.
   Disagree   Neutral   **(Agree)**

LEADERSHIP STYLE

9. I inspire people to follow me primarily through my compassion/empathy.
   No   **(Yes)**

10. I consider the company as MY company versus OUR company.
    My company   Neutral   **(Our company)**

Notes

Chapter 1

1. Howard H. Stevenson, "A Perspective on Entrepreneurship," background note 384-131, Harvard Business School, Boston, October 1983. For an interesting commentary on the durability of this definition, see Thomas R. Eisenmann, "Entrepreneurship: A Working Definition," *Harvard Business Review*, January 10, 2013, https://hbr.org/2013/01/what-is-entrepreneurship.

2. *Biography.com*, s.v. "Mark Cuban," last updated August 22, 2016, www.biography.com/people/mark-cuban-562656#synopsis.

3. Quotes from Ben Weiss in this chapter come from our interview with him on May 17, 2015.

4. *Oxford Dictionary of English*, s.v. "dynamics" (Oxford: Oxford University Press, 2009).

5. CPP, "History, Reliability and Validity of the Myers-Briggs Type Indicator® (MBTI®) Instrument," CPP, the People Development People, accessed November 15, 2016, www.cpp.com/products/mbti/mbti_info.aspx; DiSC Profile, "What Is DiSC®? The DiSC Personality Test Explained," accessed November 15, 2016, www.discprofile.com/what-is-disc/overview/; Hogan Assessments, home page, accessed November 15, 2016, www.hoganassessments.com.

6. Geoffrey A. Moore, *Crossing the Chasm: Marketing and Selling High-Tech Products to Mainstream Customers* (New York: HarperBusiness, 1999).

7. Throughout this book, you will read about highly successful business builders, most of whom we have personally interviewed. All of those builders have taken our Builder Personality Discovery questionnaire to determine their designated type. We also occasionally refer to other prominent and widely known entrepreneurs, both living and dead, to illustrate points along the way. In those cases, we have relied on publicly available and reputable sources, such as autobiographies, biographies, and contemporary media interviews to develop a sense of how those individuals probably map to our typology.

8. Harry McCracken, "How Facebook Keeps Scaling Its Culture," *Fast Company*, November 24, 2015, www.fastcompany.com/3053776/behind-the-brand/how-facebook-keeps-scaling-its-culture.

9. David Packard, *The HP Way: How Bill Hewlett and I Built Our Company* (New York: HarperBusiness, 1995).

10. See, for example, Naomi L. Quenk, *Beside Ourselves: Our Hidden Personality in Everyday Life* (Palo Alto, CA: Davis-Black, 1993).

Chapter 2

1. Unless otherwise noted, material for this chapter relies on interviews we conducted with Ben Weiss, Rick Greenberg, Len Pagon, Bob Kocher, Howard Lerman, Mi Jong Lee, Steve Breitman, Adam Jackson, and Matt Blumberg between the spring and fall of 2015. Quotes from Laurie Spengler are from an interview in November, 2014.

2. For more about Charlie Cawley's life and career, see Sam Roberts, "Charles M. Cawley, Credit Card Pioneer, Dies at 75," *New York Times*, November 24, 2015, www.nytimes.com/2015/11/25/business/charles-m-cawley-founder-of-mbna-corp-dies-at-75.html; and *Reference for Business*, s.v. "Charles M. Cawley," accessed November 15, 2016, www.referenceforbusiness.com/biography/A-E/Cawley-Charles-M-1941.html.

3. This concept and phrase comes from the classic book of the same title: Clayton M. Christensen, *The Innovator's Dilemma: When New Technologies Cause Great Firms to Fail* (Boston: Harvard Business School Press, 1997).

Chapter 3

1. Unless otherwise noted, material for this chapter relies on interviews we conducted with Brian O'Kelley, Grace Choi, Tom Phillips, Derek Lidow, Mark Bonfigli, Chris Pinkham, Brian Coester, and Bryan Roberts between the spring and fall of 2015.

2. Susie Moore, "What Sara Blakely Wished She Knew in Her 20s," *Marie Claire*, November 4, 2014, www.marieclaire.com/politics/news/a11508/sara-blakely-interview.

3. Bruce Rogers, "Tom Leighton's Journey from MIT Professor to Akamai CEO," *Forbes*, May 20, 2014, www.forbes.com/sites/brucerogers/2014/05/20/tom-leightons-journey-from-mit-professor-to-akamai-ceo/#17fc60ee1d18.

4. Carl Brooks, "Amazon's Early Efforts at Cloud Computing? Partly Accidental," June 17, 2010, https://goo.gl/8J3HUL, (accessed November 15, 2016).

Chapter 4

1. See, for example, Kim Masters, "Jessica Alba's Tears on Her Way to Building a $1 Billion Business," *Hollywood Reporter*, October 3, 2014, www .hollywoodreporter.com/features/jessica-albas-tears-her-way-736714; Celia Fernandez, "Jessica Alba Talks $1 Billion Empire," *Latina*, May 22, 2015, www .latina.com/entertainment/celebrity/jessica-alba-talks-honest-company-empire; and Clare O'Connor, "How Jessica Alba Built a $1 Billion Company, and $200 Million Fortune, Selling Parents Peace of Mind," *Forbes*, June 15, 2015, www .forbes.com/sites/clareoconnor/2015/05/27/how-jessica-alba-built-a-1-billion-company-and-200-million-fortune-selling-parents-peace-of-mind/#154765441f0c.

2. For more about Jack Dorsey and his trajectory, see, for example, *Biography .com*, s.v. "Jack Dorsey," last updated October 14, 2015, www.biography.com/ people/jack-dorsey-578280#creation-of-twitter; and Nicholas Carlson, "Jack Dorsey Is Not Steve Jobs," *Business Insider*, November 29, 2014, www.businessin sider.com/jack-dorsey-is-not-steve-jobs-2014-11.

3. Unless otherwise noted, material in this chapter relies on interviews we conducted with Derek Newell, Nate Morris, Katherine Hays, Jim Hornthal, James Currier, Angelo Pizzagalli, Ben Cohen, Jerry Greenfield, Jenny Fleiss, Christina Seelye, Greg Titus, Umair Khan, Doris Yeh, Aaron Levie, and Marsha Firestone between the spring and fall of 2015.

Chapter 5

1. Unless otherwise noted, material for this chapter relies on interviews we conducted with Margery Kraus, John Crowley, Mark Coopersmith, Peter Arvai, Suri Suriyakumar, Cindy Monroe, Chris Dries, June Ressler, and Chris Bischof between the spring and fall of 2015. Our interviews with George McLaughlin and Paul Gilbert took place in the fall of 2014 and 2013, respectively.

2. For more about Jack Ma, his trajectory as an entrepreneur, and his approach to building, see, for example, Jack Ma, "'Unparalleled Ruthlessness' Awaits: Jack Ma's Letter to Alibaba Employees," *Wall Street Journal*, May 7, 2014, http://blogs .wsj.com/chinarealtime/2014/05/07/unparalleled-ruthlessness-awaits-jack-mas-letter-to-alibaba-employees/; Jack Ma, as told to Rebecca Fannin, "How I Did It: Jack Ma, Alibaba.com," *Inc.*, January 1, 2008, www.inc.com/ magazine/20080101/how-i-did-it-jack-ma-alibaba.html; and "Jack Ma: 'To Win in the 21st Century, You Must Empower Others,'" *Project Pengyou*, January 28, 2015, http://projectpengyou.org/jack-ma-to-win-in-the-21st-century-you-must-empower-others.

3. For a fascinating after-the-fact critique of Nokia's decision-making culture, see Quy Huy and Timo Vuori, "Who Killed Nokia? Nokia Did," *INSEAD Knowledge*, September 22, 2015, http://knowledge.insead.edu/strategy/who-killed-nokia-nokia-did-4268.

4. For more on the institute, see Great Place to Work United States, "About Us," accessed November 15, 2016, www.greatplacetowork.com/about-us.

Chapter 6

1. For more on these cobuilders, see Julie Rice, "The Secrets to a Successful Business Partnership," *Fast Company*, June 18, 2015, www.fastcompany.com/3047361/hit-the-ground-running/the-secrets-to-a-successful-business-partnership; and SoulCycle, "Our Story," accessed November 15, 2016, www.soul-cycle.com/our-story/.

2. Dharmesh Shah, "Startup Insights from Paul English, Co-Founder of Kayak," *OnStartups* (blog), May 10, 2010, http://onstartups.com/tabid/3339/bid/12604/Startup-Insights-From-Paul-English-Co-Founder-of-Kayak.aspx.

3. An interesting personal observation on the Driver coauthors in this regard: one of us (John) prefers coequal frameworks in his venture activity because he feels that maximizes alignment between the parties and forces compromise when necessary; while the other (Chris) tends to view them as exceptions to his usual approach, believing that in order to win in competitive markets, a single person must have the tiebreaker vote in tough decisions.

4. Michael Abbott, "Founder Stories: Airbnb's Nate Blecharczyk on Being the Only Engineer for the First Year," *TechCrunch*, June 19, 2013, https://techcrunch.com/2013/06/19/founder-stories-airbnbs-nate-blecharczyk-on-being-the-only-engineer-for-the-first-year.

5. Special thanks to our University of California Berkeley faculty colleague, Dan Mulhern, for suggesting this approach to what he calls "paired leaders."

6. Guy Kawasaki, "How to Find a Co-Founder," *Guy Kawasaki* (blog), February 21, 2015, http://guykawasaki.com/how-to-find-a-co-founder/.

Chapter 8

1. Paul Maeder, interview with authors, October 1, 2015.

2. Andy Rachleff, interview with authors, August 4, 2015.

Chapter 9

1. Quotes from John Crowley, interview with authors, April 28, 2015.
2. Quotes from Paul Maeder, interview with authors, October 1, 2015.
3. Quotes from Laurie Spengler, interview with authors, November 4, 2014.

Appendix A

1. We chose the "3 + 3" threshold for several reasons. First, most major research reports on startup success and failure tend to concentrate on the first three to five years of a business. Second, the best available data on business scale suggests that the vast majority of startups do not surpass the $3 million threshold. Third, in light of those factors, we considered this 3 + 3 standard to be both practical and aspirational. As thousands more builders who satisfy this threshold complete our Builder Personality Discovery instrument, we expect to be able to refine it and perhaps make it more granular, for example, by industry sector or gender.

2. Gallup Strengths Center, home page, accessed November 15, 2016, www.gallupstrengthscenter.com.

3. Jim Clifton and Sangeeta Bharadwaj Badal, *Entrepreneurial StrengthsFinder 2.0* (New York: Gallup Press, 2014).

Index

Acknowledgments

Some of the original ideas that underpin this book came from the extraordinary men and women who helped build Rosetta. These include Chris's cofounder, Kurt Holstein (Explorer), whose analytical marketing gifts and passion to discover more actionable insights was critical to shaping and scaling Rosetta's service offering; Hari Mahadevan (Crusader), whose consulting and leadership gifts inspired clients and colleagues, allowing the firm to deepen its impact; and later in the journey, Nigel Adams (Crusader), who demonstrated the power of integrating business and leadership skills for greater impact. Each of these enormously talented individuals played a key role in building this book's foundation, and we are deeply grateful to all of them.

In addition, we are indebted to Rosetta's launch team—George Tang (Captain), Jason Whitney (Explorer), Chetna Bansal (Explorer), and Lawrence Choi (Explorer)—who first codified our Personality-Based Clustering technique, while Lawrence returned in the final stages of our work to fine tune some of the underlying analytics. Gifted leaders like Ned Elton (Crusader) and Shannon Hartley (Driver) helped bring the Rosetta vision to leading marketers globally. And finally, Tom Adamski (the model Captain)—taken from us well before his time—encouraged and enabled the earliest stages of the journey that became this book. Thank you, Tom.

ACKNOWLEDGMENTS

Chetna Bansal and Alyssa Pemberton led the Rosetta team that included Sarah Martin, Steven Yum, and Loren Taylor-Raymond in applying Personality-Based Clustering to the research data for this book. Thank you all.

In the early stages of our work we were helped by many people. Peter Wendell, Marsha Firestone, Ken Traub, Adam Eiseman, Taylor Francis, and Paul Chamberlain were generous with both their time and their networks, as were the Pennsylvania and New Jersey chapters of the Young Presidents' Association, and many others. Our preliminary interviews with several savvy entrepreneurs helped shape our thinking: thanks to Alexander Jutkovitz, Brian Halligan, Carol Head, Chinwe Onyeagoro, Frank Dombroski, Jay Gould, Justin Mares, Mark Buller, Paul Chachko, Neil Grimmer, and Tracy Doyle.

We are grateful to Stephanie Sandberg, Whitney Frith, and Dan Gerasmowicz, who contributed research, advice, and interview help as well. Devansh Gupta added research and write-ups, demonstrating wisdom and insight well beyond his years, complemented with help from Jenna Rodrigues, Max Bressler, Stephanie McGill, and Alex Ferguson. Heather Vanselous, our tenacious assistant, orchestrated our schedules, oversaw transcriptions, and managed many of the mission-critical aspects of our work behind the scenes.

We thank our team of initial reviewers—Gigi Goldman, Bob Kocher, Tom Higgins, Sylvia Sze, Jim Goldman, and others—who gave us candid feedback that sharpened our message. Dana Baker-Williams provided editing clarity during this key phase.

We write extensively about fit in these pages. Nowhere has the importance of that concept been more evident than in our fit as authors with our superb Harvard Business Review Press publishing team, led by Melinda Merino and supported by Jen Waring, Stephani Finks, Patty Boyd, Kenzie Travers, and Karen Palmer. Our book marketing team is led by Erin Byrne, with Margery Kraus, Jim Moorhead, and Kevin Goldman from APCO, along with Raeva Kumar's incomparable support, and by input from Chris Danner and Bob Caruso. Their excellent counterparts at HBRP include Keith Pfeffer, Julie Devoll, Nina Nocciolino, Lindsey Dietrich, Brian Galvin, Sally Ashworth, Jon Shipley, and Aniruddh Kashyap.

We were also served by a series of very helpful individuals and companies. Will Danner, Kevin Haag, George Friborg, and Nik Schulz provided design help on our website and in these pages; and Research Now, Folio3, Absolute Data, Brian Hasenkamp of Asenka Interactive, Urban Mouse, Michael Franzyshen of Ascendant Technologies, and Princeton Transcription supported us in other valuable ways.

Writing a book is a disruptive process, and ours has been no exception. Our associates at Berkeley and Princeton were wonderfully accommodating to our various requests, meetings, calls, and schedule interruptions. They include faculty colleagues Mark Coopersmith, Dan Mulhern, Whitney Hischier, and Dean Rich Lyons at UC Berkeley, as well as Benedikt Westrick, John Molner, and Fanni Fan at Rosemark. At Princeton University, the Keller Center was in our court from day one, including Ed Zschau, Derek Lidow, and Mung Chiang on the faculty side, and Cornelia Huellstrunk, Victoria Dorman, Beth Jarvie, Stephanie Landers, and JD Jasper, among others, on the staff.

We were very fortunate to have the wise counsel of our agent, Jim Levine, of the Levine, Greenberg, Rostan Literary Agency, and the continued support of dear friends Treby Williams, Dannie Kennedy, and Tom Higgins.

As we review this list, incomplete as it no doubt is, we are humbled by the help we have received from so many people. However, lastly and most importantly, we thank our wives, Leslie and Peach, whose patience, judgment, and emotional support was immeasurable. Without them, this book simply would never have been possible.

Chris Kuenne and John Danner
December 11, 2016

About the Authors

This book crystallized unexpectedly over lunch in December 2014. We thought we were going to talk about our respective classes at Princeton the prior semester. But as we began comparing notes about our various careers, ideas, and interests, we realized how convergent yet complementary they were. We were both fascinated by why and how entrepreneurs create something from nothing, building businesses that grow from startups into successful enterprises, and we were both convinced of the importance of that process in a world looking for greater economic opportunity and social progress. In that context, Chris had long been intrigued by the dimension of how personality shapes behavior in marketplaces, and John by the issues and challenges of innovation and leadership.

We both felt that no one had yet decoded the interplay between the *who* and the *how* at the core of the entrepreneurial process: the catalytic interaction between the business founder's own personality and the various challenges he or she must confront in building a great enterprise. In short, we thought who you are must shape how you build.

Sometimes serendipity trumps strategy. From that casual conversation came the partnership and friendship that led to this book. In the process of conducting our research, honing our ideas, and writing these chapters, we've integrated our respective East and West Coast styles of thinking and working—so much so that we nicknamed our collaboration "West by Northeast."

Here's a more formal snapshot of our respective backgrounds.

Chris Kuenne, founder of Rosetta and Rosemark Capital, is a highly successful entrepreneur, member of Princeton University's faculty, and growth capital investor. For more than thirty years he has been fascinated by the question of what motivates people to act as they do in a commercial context. He has devoted his career to translating insights about customer motivation into personalized sales and marketing techniques that accelerate enterprise growth.

Chris is now focused, with his colleagues at Rosemark, on applying these growth techniques to investments in partnership with leading private equity firms. He is a frequent speaker to various business leadership audiences, including the Young Presidents' Organization (YPO), venture capital associations, the Association for Corporate Growth (ACG), and the CFO Roundtable, among many others. He is an active contributor to *Forbes* and a range of other leading industry magazines and journals, such as *Advertising Age*, *Banking Strategies*, and *Pharmaceutical Executive*. He has also appeared on CNBC's *Street Signs*, *Forbes* podcasts, and other media outlets.

Prior to founding Rosetta, Chris co-led the retail marketing practice at First Manhattan Consulting Group, following ten years in marketing management at Johnson & Johnson, where he led the Band-Aid and Tylenol brand franchises. Chris serves on various corporate and nonprofit boards. He received his MBA with honors from Harvard Business School, and his BA from Princeton University. He lives in Princeton, New Jersey, and Shelburne, Vermont, with his wife, Leslie, and their three sons, Peter, William, and Matthew.

John Danner teaches, consults, speaks, and writes about innovation, entrepreneurship, strategy, and leadership. He has always been intrigued by how these elements converge to create economic and social value across the private, nonprofit, and government sectors, and his career as an executive, entrepreneur, and adviser spans all three domains.

Currently, as Senior Fellow of UC Berkeley's Institute for Business Innovation and Lester Center for Entrepreneurship, John teaches at the Haas School of Business. Each fall he is also a visiting professor in entrepreneurship at Princeton. In addition to his consulting practice, he conducts executive education and leadership courses in the United States and around the world. A popular speaker at conferences globally, he originated the idea for TED U[niversity], appearing most recently on the TEDx Beacon and TEDx Athens stages.

John serves on several advisory boards and judges the international Spark Design Awards. He has been covered in the *New York Times*, *Wall Street Journal*, *Financial Times*, *Fortune*, *Fast Company*, *Chief Executive*, *Strategy + Business*, *Entrepreneur*, and *Business Insider*, as well as various foreign media. He is the coauthor of *The Other "F" Word: How Smart Leaders, Teams, and Entrepreneurs Put Failure to Work*.

John holds JD, MPH, and MEd degrees from UC Berkeley and a BA cum laude from Harvard College. He lives in Berkeley, California, and New York City with his wife, Nancy Pietrafesa, with whom he has three sons, Eliot, Chris, and Will.

You can reach the authors using the following methods:

Chris Kuenne
chris.kuenne@rosemark.com
www.rosemark.com
linkedin.com/in/chriskuenne
@kuenne_chris

John Danner
danner@berkeley.edu
www.johndanner.com
linkedin.com/in/johndanner1
@dannerjd

www.builtforgrowth.com